GoodHousekeeping

BLEND IT!

GoodHousekeeping

BLEND IT!

150 SENSATIONAL RECIPES TO MAKE IN YOUR BLENDER

HEARST BOOKS
A division of Sterling Publishing Co., Inc.

New York / London
www.sterlingpublishing.com

GOOD HOUSEKEEPING

Rosemary Ellis **Editor in Chief**
Susan Westmoreland **Food Director**
Samantha Cassetty **Nutrition Director**
Sharon Franke **Food Appliances Director**

BOOK DESIGN BY Memo Productions
PHOTOGRAPHY CREDITS
All Photography by Theresa Raffetto with
the following exceptions: Ann Stratton: pages 99,
108, 111, and 125. Brian Hagiwara: pages 152 and
159. Rita Maas: pages 33 and 131.
Mark Thomas: Page 173.
COVER CREDITS
FRONT COVER: Foodcollection/Getty Images
SPINE: Theresa Raffetto
BACK COVER: (clockwise from top left): Theresa
Raffetto; Ann Stratton; Theresa Raffetto

Library of Congress
Cataloging-in-Publication Data
Blend it! : 150 sensational recipes to make
in your blender / from the editors of
Good Housekeeping.
            p. cm.
    1. Blenders (Cookery) 2. Smoothies (Beverages)
3. Cocktails. 4. Soups 5. Dips (Appetizers)
6. Pancakes, waffles, etc. I. Good housekeeping
(New York, N.Y.)
    TX840.B5.B45 2003
    641.5'89--dc21   2003001566

10 9 8 7 6 5 4 3 2 1

The Good Housekeeping Cookbook Seal
guarantees that the recipes in this cookbook meet
the strict standards of the Good Housekeeping
Research Institute. The Institute has been a
source of reliable information and a consumer
advocate since 1900, and established its seal of
approval in 1909. Every recipe has been triple-
tested for ease, reliability, and great taste.

Published by Hearst Books
A Division of Sterling Publishing Co., Inc.
387 Park Avenue South, New York, NY 10016

Good Housekeeping is a registered trademark
of Hearst Communications, Inc.

www.goodhousekeeping.com

For information about custom editions, special
sales, premium and corporate purchases, please
contact Sterling Special Sales Department at 800-
805-5489 or specialsales@sterlingpublishing.com.

Distributed in Canada by Sterling Publishing
c/o Canadian Manda Group, 165 Dufferin Street
Toronto, Ontario, Canada M6K 3H6

Distributed in Australia by Capricorn Link
(Australia) Pty. Ltd.
P.O. Box 704, Windsor, NSW 2756 Australia

Manufactured in China

Sterling ISBN 978-1-58816-807-8

CONTENTS

FOREWORD

Fun! We had a lot of it creating the recipes for *Blend It!* and we want you to have a lot of fun making them. And why not? The blender makes it easy to cook just about anything—simply press the button and buzz. There's little cleanup and most of the recipes are so simple, even kids will want to help with the cooking. Better yet, almost every recipe in this book is a treat by anyone's definition—luscious smoothies, sinfully rich soda fountain frappes, creamy soups, tender pancakes, and some very delicious frozen cocktails.

Blend It! also addresses the needs of today's woman on the go, who is short on time but still wants to make delicious, nutritious food for her family. If you want to get the kids off to school in minutes, give them one of our creamy smoothies made with yogurt, milk, or soy milk. They are protein-packed and flavorful. Imagine starting the day with a Blueberry Blast or Breakfast Jumpstart!

Looking for a special treat to share with the ones you love? Indulge them with a Double-Chocolate Malted, Classic Vanilla Milkshake, or Root Beer Float. For an afternoon pick-me-up, try our Frosty Cappuccino and Mocha Frappa Cinno—we think they're just as good as their coffee bar rivals.

Wouldn't it be fun to be able to make colorful cocktails just like the ones at your favorite watering hole? Fizzes, Slushes & Frozen Cocktails is where you'll discover how easy it is to prepare daiquiris, margaritas, and piña coladas, plus sensational nonalcoholic beverages such as our Frozen Virgin Mary and Frozen Iced Tea.

Your blender will make quick work of fixing soup, too. You'll find smooth silky-textured soups, like Cream of Asparagus or Butternut-Apple, as well as thick, chunky soups, like Split-Pea Soup with Ham and hearty Potato Soup with Bacon and Parmesan.

You'll also discover how easy it is to make a perfect, foolproof Hollandaise Sauce and to wow guests at the next potluck party with Mango Curry Dip to start and Sublime Chocolate Sauce for dessert.

Last, but not least, you'll find that the blender is great for whipping up batters for pancakes, popovers, and waffles. For breakfast, let your family feast on our easy Puffy Pancake, Whole-Grain Waffles, or Cheese Blintzes. For dinner, you'll find that light, airy Popovers are a snap to make and delicious with roast meats. For dessert, try the Cherry-Almond Clafouti or our easy crepes.

So get ready to enjoy some of the easiest, most delicious recipes you ever tasted—with just the push of a button—it's that simple. It's also fun—so why not get started now!

SUSAN WESTMORELAND
Food Director, *Good Housekeeping*

Roasted Red Pepper and Walnut Dip (page 122)

THE BUZZ ON BLENDERS

Icy cold drinks, velvety soups, creamy soda fountain treats—you can make them all quickly and easily in the blender with just the flick of the wrist. However, to ensure perfect results every time, and for safety's sake, it helps to know a little bit about how your blender works and to follow a few simple food-preparation guidelines.

Speeding Permitted

All blenders feature a control panel offering several speed options. Some models have four or five speeds, others just high and low; still other manufacturers list methods rather than speed, such as whip, puree, liquefy, chop. But rest assured—you can make any recipe in this book in any standard blender using the high button, which blends foods quickly and smoothly. If your blender has a puree button, which is more powerful, use it for making thicker mixtures such as soups and dips. You can use the high button for soups and dips, too—it will just take a bit longer.

Safety Does It

- Always keep your hand on top of the blender while it is in use as a precaution against the top coming off unexpectedly. This can happen if you've added too many ingredients at one time or they create more volume than you anticipated.
- Be sure the motor is off before you clean down the sides of the blender and move the food onto the blades. Use a rubber spatula only—not a metal one or a knife.
- Never put your fingers in the container. The blades are sharp.

Blend It Better

Whether you're making a silky-smooth soup or a grainy frozen slush, the goal when blending is always the same—consistent texture.

- Add the food in small batches. This will ensure that your ingredients get uniformly pureed and keep the blender from overflowing.
- Chill the ingredients before making blender drinks. This will keep your drinks cold longer and create a smoother texture.
- Cut pieces of fruit and vegetables into small uniform sizes. This gives better consistency and puts less strain on the blender motor.

- Place equal parts liquid and solid foods in the blender when pureeing soups. This will keep the texture consistent from one batch to the next.
- For best texture, let hot liquids cool slightly before adding them to the blender.
- Always crush ice or break it into in small cubes before adding it to the container, particularly if your blender has a less powerful motor.
- If you are blending ice with other ingredients, add ice to blender last.

Buying a New Blender

Once you discover the wonderful variety of luscious smoothies, frozen drinks, soups, and pancakes that can be made in the blender you may want to buy a newer, bigger, and more powerful model. If so, check them out carefully before you make your purchase.

- Look for a blender that has a sturdy base to keep it stable. This will prevent it from jumping around on the counter while in use.
- Check the capacity of the glass container. A smaller (32-ounce) container is fine if you will be making just one smoothie or drink at a time. However, opt for a 40-ounce container if you plan to whip up two drinks at a time or blend soup and pancake batters.
- Consider paying extra for a more powerful motor, particularly if you will be making slushes and frozen cocktails. Many of the newer blenders have 330- to 400-watt motors that make crushing ice a snap.

SMOOTHIES & BLENDER BREAKFASTS

Strawberry Mania (page 15)

BANANA-STRAWBERRY BREAKFAST SMOOTHIE

A classic smoothie combination and a great breakfast. For added flavor, use one of the orange juice blends, such as orange-strawberry.

ACTIVE TIME: 5 MINUTES · **TOTAL TIME:** 5 MINUTES
MAKES: 1½ CUPS OR 1 SERVING

½ CUP ORANGE JUICE, CHILLED

¾ CUP FROZEN STRAWBERRIES

1 BANANA, SLICED

In blender, combine orange juice, strawberries, and banana and blend until mixture is smooth. Pour into 1 tall glass.

EACH SERVING: ABOUT 203 CALORIES | 3 G PROTEIN | 51 G CARBOHYDRATE | 1 G TOTAL FAT (0 G SATURATED) | 0 MG CHOLESTEROL | 5 MG SODIUM

ROSY PEAR-CRANBERRY SMOOTHIE

Using canned pears makes this refreshing drink a snap to prepare.

ACTIVE TIME: 5 MINUTES · **TOTAL TIME:** 5 MINUTES
MAKES: 1½ CUPS OR 1 SERVING

½ CUP CRANBERRY JUICE COCKTAIL, CHILLED

2 CANNED PEAR HALVES IN LIGHT SYRUP, CHILLED, DRAINED

4 ICE CUBES

In blender, combine cranberry juice cocktail and pear halves and blend until mixture is smooth. With the motor running, add the ice cubes one at a time and blend until smooth. Pour into 1 tall glass.

EACH SERVING: ABOUT 203 CALORIES | 3 G PROTEIN | 51 G CARBOHYDRATE | 1 G TOTAL FAT (0 G SATURATED) | 0 MG CHOLESTEROL | 5 MG SODIUM

ORANGE SUNRISE

What a way to start the day! If you don't have soy milk you can substitute low-fat milk or buttermilk.

ACTIVE TIME: 5 MINUTES · **TOTAL TIME:** 5 MINUTES
MAKES: 1¾ CUPS OR 1 SERVING

- 1 CUP VANILLA SOY MILK
- ¼ CUP FROZEN ORANGE JUICE CONCENTRATE
- 2 TABLESPOONS ORANGE MARMALADE
- 2 ICE CUBES

In blender, combine soy milk, orange juice concentrate, marmalade, and ice and blend until mixture is smooth and frothy. Pour into 1 tall glass.

EACH SERVING: ABOUT 360 CALORIES | 8 G PROTEIN | 73 G CARBOHYDRATE | 5 G TOTAL FAT (0 G SATURATED) | 0 MG CHOLESTEROL | 144 MG SODIUM

BREAKFAST JUMPSTART

As healthy a morning lift off as you could find! This luscious blend of soy milk, fruits, and a sprinkling of wheat germ is loaded with vitamins and minerals to get you going.

ACTIVE TIME: 5 MINUTES · **TOTAL TIME:** 5 MINUTES PLUS FREEZING
MAKES: 2 CUPS OR 1 SERVING

- 1 CUP SOY MILK
- 1 FROZEN BANANA, SLICED
- 1 CUP STRAWBERRIES, HULLED
- 2 TABLESPOONS WHEAT GERM
- 1 TABLESPOON HONEY

In blender, combine soy milk, banana, strawberries, wheat germ, and honey and blend until mixture is smooth and frothy. Pour into 1 tall glass.

EACH SERVING: ABOUT 342 CALORIES | 13 G PROTEIN | 66 G CARBOHYDRATE | 7 G TOTAL FAT (1 G SATURATED) | 0 MG CHOLESTEROL | 33 MG SODIUM

TROPICAL MANGO SMOOTHIE

Paradise in a glass. Make it with a firm ripe banana for best flavor.

ACTIVE TIME: 10 MINUTES · **TOTAL TIME:** 10 MINUTES

MAKES: 2 CUPS OR 1 SERVING

½ CUP PINEAPPLE JUICE, CHILLED

1 CUP DICED MANGO

1 BANANA, SLICED

2 TEASPOONS FRESH LIME JUICE

½ TEASPOON GRATED PEELED FRESH GINGER

3 ICE CUBES

In blender, combine pineapple juice, mango, banana, lime juice, ginger, and ice and blend until mixture is smooth. Pour into 1 tall glass.

EACH SERVING: ABOUT 289 CALORIES │ 3 G PROTEIN │ 74 G CARBOHYDRATE │ 1 G TOTAL FAT (0 G SATURATED │ 0 MG CHOLESTEROL │ 6 MG SODIUM

STRAWBERRY MANIA

A double dose of strawberries makes this pink drink doubly delicious.

ACTIVE TIME: 5 MINUTES · **TOTAL TIME:** 5 MINUTES
MAKES: 1¾ CUPS OR 1 SERVING

¼ CUP CRANBERRY JUICE COCKTAIL, CHILLED

1 CONTAINER (8 OUNCES) LOW-FAT STRAWBERRY YOGURT

1 CUP FROZEN STRAWBERRIES

In blender, combine cranberry juice, yogurt, and strawberries and blend until mixture is smooth and frothy. Pour into 1 tall glass.

EACH SERVING: ABOUT 326 CALORIES | 10 G PROTEIN | 68 G CARBOHYDRATE | 4 G TOTAL FAT (2 G SATURATED) | 15 MG CHOLESTEROL | 141 MG SODIUM

Cantaloupe-Lime Smoothie

CANTALOUPE-LIME SMOOTHIE

Double your pleasure and make two. Garnish with a fresh slice of lime.

ACTIVE TIME: 10 MINUTES · **TOTAL TIME:** 10 MINUTES
MAKES: 2 CUPS OR 1 SERVING

---

1   LIME

2   CUPS DICED CANTALOUPE

⅓ CUP DICED PEACH

1   TABLESPOON HONEY

3   ICE CUBES

1   From lime, grate ½ teaspoon peel and squeeze 2 tablespoons juice.
2   In blender, combine lime peel, lime juice, cantaloupe, peach, honey, and ice and blend until mixture is smooth and frothy. Pour into 1 tall glass.

EACH SERVING: ABOUT 233 CALORIES | 4 G PROTEIN | 60 G CARBOHYDRATE | 1 G TOTAL FAT (0 G SATURATED) | 0 MG CHOLESTEROL | 30 MG SODIUM

PAPAYA PUNCH

This papaya-packed punch is rich in beta-carotene.

ACTIVE TIME: 10 MINUTES · **TOTAL TIME:** 10 MINUTES
MAKES: 1½ CUPS OR 1 SERVING

---

1   CUP PAPAYA NECTAR OR ORANGE JUICE, CHILLED

1   CUP DICED PAPAYA

1   TABLESPOON FRESH LIME JUICE

1   TO 2 TEASPOONS SUGAR

1   DROP COCONUT EXTRACT

3   ICE CUBES

In blender, combine papaya nectar, papaya, lime juice, sugar, coconut extract, and ice and blend until mixture is smooth. Pour into 1 tall glass.

EACH SERVING: ABOUT 232 CALORIES | 1 G PROTEIN | 59 G CARBOHYDRATE | 1 G TOTAL FAT (0 G SATURATED) | 0 MG CHOLESTEROL | 17 MG SODIUM

HONEYDEW-KIWI COOLER

A refreshing mixture of melon and kiwi that's also good for you. Kiwis have even more vitamin C than oranges.

ACTIVE TIME: 10 MINUTES · **TOTAL TIME:** 10 MINUTES
MAKES: 2 CUPS OR 1 SERVING

2 CUPS DICED HONEYDEW MELON	3 ICE CUBES
1 TABLESPOON FRESH LEMON JUICE	½ CUP FROZEN DICED KIWI
1 TABLESPOON HONEY	

In blender, combine honeydew, lemon juice, honey, and ice and blend until smooth. Add kiwi and blend until kiwi is broken up, but the seeds are not ground. Pour into 1 tall glass.

EACH SERVING: ABOUT 246 CALORIES | 3 G PROTEIN | 64 G CARBOHYDRATE | 1 G TOTAL FAT (0 G SATURATED) | 0 MG CHOLESTEROL | 41 MG SODIUM

GINGER-PEACH BLUSH

This sensational smoothie gets its gorgeous color from peaches and raspberries and its zip from candied ginger.

ACTIVE TIME: 5 MINUTES · **TOTAL TIME:** 5 MINUTES
MAKES: 1¾ CUPS OR 1 SERVING

1 CUP PEACH NECTAR, CHILLED	¼ CUP FROZEN RASPBERRIES
1 CUP FROZEN SLICED PEACHES	2 TEASPOONS MINCED CRYSTALLIZED GINGER

In blender, combine peach nectar, peaches, raspberries, and ginger and blend until mixture is smooth. Pour into 1 tall glass.

EACH SERVING: ABOUT 244 CALORIES | 2 G PROTEIN | 63 G CARBOHYDRATE | 0 G TOTAL FAT (0 SATURATED) | 0 MG CHOLESTEROL | 19 MG SODIUM

Honeydew-Kiwi Cooler

APPLE-BANANA SMOOTHIE

Here's an easy and delicious way to get your apple a day and keep the doctor away. We used a Granny Smith, but you could substitute a Golden Delicious or Gala, if you prefer.

ACTIVE TIME: 10 MINUTES · **TOTAL TIME:** 10 MINUTES PLUS FREEZING

MAKES: 2 CUPS OR 1 SERVING

¾ CUP APPLE JUICE, CHILLED

¼ CUP FROZEN APPLE JUICE CONCENTRATE

⅓ CUP APPLESAUCE

1 CUP FROZEN DICED GRANNY SMITH APPLE

½ FROZEN BANANA, SLICED

PINCH GROUND CARDAMOM

In a blender, combine apple juice, apple juice concentrate, applesauce, diced apple, banana, and cardamom and blend until mixture is smooth. Pour into 1 tall glass.

EACH SERVING: ABOUT 387 CALORIES │ 1 G PROTEIN │ 98 G CARBOHYDRATE │ 1 G TOTAL FAT (0 G SATURATED) │ 0 MG CHOLESTEROL │ 26 MG SODIUM

CHOCOLATE-BANANA SMOOTHIE

Kids love the combo of chocolate and bananas, and it's so easy to make, they can do it themselves.

ACTIVE TIME: 5 MINUTES · **TOTAL TIME:** 5 MINUTES PLUS FREEZING
MAKES: 2 CUPS OR 1 SERVING

1	FROZEN BANANA, SLICED	3	TO 4 TABLESPOONS CHOCOLATE SYRUP
¾	CUP MILK	3	TO 4 ICE CUBES

In blender, combine banana, milk, chocolate syrup, and ice and blend until mixture is smooth and frothy. Pour into 1 tall glass.

EACH SERVING: ABOUT 430 CALORIES | 9 G PROTEIN, 85 G CARBOHYDRATE | 8 G TOTAL FAT (4 G SATURATED) | 25 MG CHOLESTEROL | 145 MG SODIUM

BANANA BAYOU SMOOTHIE

As rich and delicious as that other Big Easy favorite—Bananas Foster.

ACTIVE TIME: 5 MINUTES · **TOTAL TIME:** 5 MINUTES PLUS FREEZING
MAKES: 1½ CUPS OR 1 SERVING

1	CUP BUTTERMILK	2	TABLESPOONS PREPARED CARAMEL SAUCE
1	FROZEN BANANA, SLICED	1	TABLESPOON CHOPPED PECANS FOR GARNISH

In blender, combine buttermilk, banana, and caramel sauce and blend until mixture is smooth and frothy. Pour into 1 tall glass and garnish with pecans.

EACH SERVING: ABOUT 384 CALORIES | 10 G PROTEIN | 71 G CARBOHYDRATE | 8 G TOTAL FAT (2 G SATURATED | 9 MG CHOLESTEROL | 368 MG SODIUM

APRICOT-RASPBERRY REFRESHER

A delicious ruby-red razzle dazzler. Top it with some fresh raspberries.

ACTIVE TIME: 5 MINUTES · **TOTAL TIME:** 5 MINUTES

MAKES: 1¾ CUPS OR 1 SERVING

1 SMALL CAN (5.5 OUNCES) APRICOT NECTAR, CHILLED (⅔ CUP)

½ CAN (15 OUNCES) APRICOT HALVES IN LIGHT SYRUP, DRAINED (7 TO 8 HALVES)

3 ICE CUBES

1 TABLESPOON HONEY

¼ CUP FROZEN RASPBERRIES

In blender, combine apricot nectar, apricot halves, ice, and honey and blend until mixture is smooth. Add raspberries and blend until broken up but not completely blended in. Pour into 1 tall glass.

EACH SERVING: ABOUT 262 CALORIES | 2 G PROTEIN | 68 G CARBOHYDRATE | 0 G TOTAL FAT (0 G SATURATED) | 0 MG CHOLESTEROL | 12 MG SODIUM

MANGO-PEACH BATIDO

Batidos are Latino smoothies or milkshakes. For a lower-fat version, substitute low-fat sweetened condensed milk.

ACTIVE TIME: 10 MINUTES · **TOTAL TIME:** 10 MINUTES

MAKES 2 CUPS OR 1 SERVING

⅓ CUP WATER

¼ CUP SWEETENED CONDENSED MILK

3 TABLESPOONS FRESH LIME JUICE

1 CUP DICED MANGO

1 CUP FROZEN SLICED PEACHES OR NECTARINES

4 ICE CUBES

In blender, combine water, condensed milk, lime juice, mango, peaches, and ice and blend until mixture is smooth and frothy. Pour into 1 tall glass.

EACH SERVING: ABOUT 440 CALORIES | 9 G PROTEIN | 94 G CARBOHYDRATE | 7 G TOTAL FAT (4 G SATURATED) | 26 MG CHOLESTEROL | 101 MG SODIUM

CREAMY STRAWBERRY-ORANGE SMOOTHIE

This quick fix is a great way to get the kids off to school in the morning.

ACTIVE TIME: 5 MINUTES · **TOTAL TIME:** 5 MINUTES

MAKES: 1¾ CUPS OR 1 SERVING

¾ CUP ORANGE JUICE, CHILLED

¼ CUP NONFAT DRY MILK

1¼ CUPS FROZEN STRAWBERRIES

2 TABLESPOONS HONEY

2 ICE CUBES

In blender, combine orange juice, dry milk, strawberries, honey, and ice and blend until mixture is smooth. Pour into 1 tall glass.

EACH SERVING: ABOUT 338 CALORIES | 8 G PROTEIN | 80 G CARBOHYDRATE | 1 G TOTAL FAT (0 G SATURATED) | 3 MG CHOLESTEROL | 102 MG SODIUM

BLACK AND BLUEBERRY BLIZZARD

This spectacular blend is vitamin packed—and low-fat, too.

ACTIVE TIME: 5 MINUTES · **TOTAL TIME:** 5 MINUTES
MAKES: 2 CUPS OR 1 SERVING

½ CUP BUTTERMILK

½ CUP ORANGE JUICE, CHILLED

1 CUP FROZEN BLUEBERRIES

½ CUP FROZEN BLACKBERRIES

1 TABLESPOON HONEY

In blender, combine buttermilk, orange juice, blueberries, blackberries, and honey and blend until mixture is smooth and frothy. Pour into 1 tall glass.

EACH SERVING: ABOUT 287 CALORIES | 7 G PROTEIN | 64 G CARBOHYDRATE | 2 G TOTAL FAT (1 G SATURATED | 4 MG CHOLESTEROL | 141 MG SODIUM

DOUBLE-PEACH SMOOTHIE

Be sure to use juicy ripe peaches for the best flavor.

ACTIVE TIME: 5 MINUTES · **TOTAL TIME:** 5 MINUTES
MAKES: ABOUT 2¾ CUPS OR 2 SERVINGS

1 CUP PEELED, SLICED PEACHES (ABOUT 2 MEDIUM)

1 CUP PEACH JUICE OR NECTAR, CHILLED

½ CUP VANILLA LOW-FAT YOGURT

3 ICE CUBES

In blender, combine peaches, peach juice, yogurt, and ice and blend until mixture is smooth and frothy. Pour into 2 tall glasses.

EACH SERVING: ABOUT 160 CALORIES | 3 G PROTEIN | 36 G CARBOHYDRATE | 1 G TOTAL FAT (1 G SATURATED) | 3 MG CHOLESTEROL | 45 MG SODIUM

HEALTH-NUT SMOOTHIE

So good-tasting and so good for you. In addition to vitamin-rich blueberries and apples, this elixir contains flaxseed, a rich source of omega-3 fatty acids, fiber, minerals, and amino acids.

ACTIVE TIME: 10 MINUTES · **TOTAL TIME:** 10 MINUTES
MAKES: 1¾ CUPS OR 1 SERVING

1 NAVEL ORANGE	3 ICE CUBES
½ CUP PLAIN LOW-FAT YOGURT	1 TO 2 TABLESPOONS HONEY
⅔ CUP FROZEN BLUEBERRIES	1 TO 2 TABLESPOONS GROUND FLAXSEED*
½ CUP CHOPPED APPLE	GRANOLA FOR GARNISH

1 From orange, grate ½ teaspoon peel. Remove remaining peel and white pith from orange and discard. Section orange.
2 In blender, combine orange peel, orange sections, yogurt, blueberries, apple, ice, honey, and flaxseed and blend until mixture is smooth. Pour into 1 tall glass. Garnish with granola.

* **TIP** Although you can buy ground flaxseed, it's best to buy it whole so it will stay at its optimum freshness. To release the heart-healthy nutrients from its hard shell, it must be ground in a blender or in a nut or coffee grinder before it is added to the smoothie.

EACH SERVING: ABOUT 424 CALORIES | 11 G PROTEIN | 84 G CARBOHYDRATE | 7 G TOTAL FAT (2 G SATURATED) | 7 MG CHOLESTEROL | 106 MG SODIUM

MANGO-STRAWBERRY SMOOTHIE

Either way you make it—with mango or with apricot nectar—this is a wonderful combination. If you use frozen berries, skip the ice cubes.

ACTIVE TIME: 5 MINUTES · **TOTAL TIME:** 5 MINUTES

MAKES: 2½ CUPS OR 2 SERVINGS

---

1   CUP FRESH OR FROZEN UNSWEETENED STRAWBERRIES

1   CUP MANGO OR APRICOT NECTAR, CHILLED

½   CUP PLAIN OR VANILLA YOGURT

4   ICE CUBES

In blender, combine strawberries, mango nectar, yogurt, and ice and blend until mixture is smooth and frothy. Pour into 2 tall glasses. Serve with straws, if you like.

EACH SERVING: ABOUT 129 CALORIES │ 4 G PROTEIN │ 27 G CARBOHYDRATE │ 1 G TOTAL FAT (1 G SATURATED) │ 3 MG CHOLESTEROL │ 44 MG SODIUM

CHERRY-BERRY SMOOTHIE

There are many juice blends available and all would work well in this frosty drink. We used one that is a combination of carrot, apple, cherry, and three berry juices.

ACTIVE TIME: 5 MINUTES · **TOTAL TIME:** 5 MINUTES

MAKES: 2 CUPS OR 1 SERVING

½ CUP BERRY JUICE BLEND, CHILLED

1   CONTAINER (8 OUNCES) LOW-FAT
    CHERRY YOGURT

½ CUP FROZEN PITTED SWEET CHERRIES

2   ICE CUBES

In a blender, combine juice, yogurt, cherries, and ice and blend until mixture is smooth and frothy. Pour into 1 tall glass.

EACH SERVING: ABOUT 410 CALORIES | 10 G PROTEIN | 87 G CARBOHYDRATE | 3 G TOTAL FAT (2 G SATURATED) | 15 MG CHOLESTEROL | 159 MG SODIUM

PINEAPPLE-CITRUS SMOOTHIE

This golden smoothie looks and tastes like sunshine in a glass, and it's a nutritional knockout to boot. The orange juice and pineapple are high in vitamin C and the banana is a good source of potassium.

ACTIVE TIME: 5 MINUTES · **TOTAL TIME:** 5 MINUTES PLUS FREEZING
MAKES: 1¾ CUPS OR 1 SERVING

¾ CUP ORANGE-TANGERINE JUICE BLEND, CHILLED

¼ CUP CARROT JUICE, CHILLED

1 CUP FROZEN CANNED-PINEAPPLE CHUNKS

½ FROZEN BANANA, SLICED

In blender, combine orange-tangerine juice, carrot juice, pineapple, and banana and blend until mixture is smooth and frothy. Pour smoothie into 1 tall glass.

EACH SERVING: ABOUT 285 CALORIES │ 1 G PROTEIN │ 72 G CARBOHYDRATE │ 0 G TOTAL FAT (0 G SATURATED) │ 0 MG CHOLESTEROL │ 40 MG SODIUM

Blueberry Blast

BLUEBERRY BLAST

Garnish with a skewer of fresh blueberries.

ACTIVE TIME: 5 MINUTES · **TOTAL TIME:** 5 MINUTES
MAKES: 1⅓ CUPS OR 1 SERVING

¼ CUP CRANBERRY JUICE COCKTAIL,
    CHILLED

1 CONTAINER (8 OUNCES) LOW-FAT
    BLUEBERRY YOGURT

½ CUP FROZEN BLUEBERRIES

In blender, combine cranberry juice, yogurt, and blueberries and blend until mixture is smooth and frothy. Pour into 1 tall glass.

EACH SERVING: ABOUT 311 CALORIES | 10 G PROTEIN | 63 G CARBOHYDRATE | 3 G TOTAL FAT (2 G SATURATED) | 15 MG CHOLESTEROL | 146 MG SODIUM.

THREE-BERRY SMOOTHIE

Enjoy the summery taste of berries all year round.

ACTIVE TIME: 5 MINUTES · **TOTAL TIME:** 5 MINUTES
MAKES: 1¼ CUPS OR 1 SERVING

½ CUP CRANBERRY-RASPBERRY JUICE,
    CHILLED

½ CUP LOW-FAT VANILLA YOGURT

1 CUP FROZEN BERRY MEDLEY
    (STRAWBERRIES, RASPBERRIES,
    BLACKBERRIES, AND BLUEBERRIES)

2 TEASPOONS HONEY

In blender, combine cranberry-raspberry juice, yogurt, berries, and honey and blend until mixture is smooth. Pour into 1 tall glass.

EACH SERVING: ABOUT 293 CALORIES | 7 G PROTEIN | 65 G CARBOHYDRATE | 2 G TOTAL FAT (1 G SATURATED) | 8 MG CHOLESTEROL | 108 MG SODIUM

GREAT GRAPE SMOOTHIE

Here's an especially heart-healthy drink. Not only is it low in fat, but red grapes contain the same phytochemicals found in red wine that protect against heart disease.

ACTIVE TIME: 5 MINUTES · **TOTAL TIME:** 5 MINUTES PLUS FREEZING
MAKES: 1½ CUPS OR 1 SERVING

½ CUP GRAPE JUICE, CHILLED

¼ CUP PLAIN LOW-FAT YOGURT

1 CUP FROZEN SEEDLESS RED GRAPES

In blender, combine grape juice, yogurt, and grapes and blend until mixture is smooth and frothy. Pour into 1 tall glass.

EACH SERVING: ABOUT 228 CALORIES | 5 G PROTEIN | 51 G CARBOHYDRATE | 2 G TOTAL FAT (1 G SATURATED) | 4 MG CHOLESTEROL | 50 MG SODIUM

LEMON-CRANBERRY SMOOTHIE

This classy, cool combo of lemon and cranberry is perfect for a hot summer day. Garnish with julienne strips of lemon peel.

ACTIVE TIME: 10 MINUTES · **TOTAL TIME:** 10 MINUTES
MAKES: 2 CUPS OR 1 SERVING

1 TO 2 LEMONS

1 CONTAINER (8 OUNCES) LOW-FAT LEMON YOGURT

½ CUP WHOLE-BERRY CRANBERRY SAUCE, CHILLED

4 TO 5 ICE CUBES

1 From lemons, grate 1 teaspoon peel and squeeze 3 tablespoons juice.
2 In blender, combine lemon peel, lemon juice, yogurt, cranberry sauce, and ice and blend until mixture is smooth. Pour into 1 tall glass.

EACH SERVING: ABOUT 442 CALORIES | 10 G PROTEIN | 96 G CARBOHYDRATE | 3 G TOTAL FAT (2 G SATURATED) | 15 MG CHOLESTEROL | 230 MG SODIUM

Great Grape Smoothie

ICED TOMATO SMOOTHIE

Strawberries, carrot, and mango blend beautifully with tomatoes. For the best flavor use a juicy vine-ripened tomato.

ACTIVE TIME: 10 MINUTES · **TOTAL TIME:** 10 MINUTES PLUS FREEZING

MAKES: 1¾ CUPS OR 1 SERVING

¾ CUP CARROT JUICE, CHILLED	¾ CUP FROZEN STRAWBERRIES
¾ CUP DICED FROZEN TOMATO	½ CUP DICED MANGO

In blender, combine carrot juice, tomato, strawberries, and mango and blend until mixture is smooth. Pour into 1 tall glass.

EACH SERVING: ABOUT 193 CALORIES | 4 G PROTEIN | 47 G CARBOHYDRATE | 2 G TOTAL FAT (0 G SATURATED) | 0 MG CHOLESTEROL | 71 MG SODIUM

GREEN THUMB SMOOTHIE

An icy sparkler that tastes like it comes straight from the garden.

TOTAL TIME: 10 MINUTES PLUS FREEZING · **MAKES:** 1¾ CUPS OR 1 SERVING

½ CUP WHITE GRAPE JUICE, CHILLED

1   CUP FROZEN GREEN SEEDLESS GRAPES

1   CUP SEEDED, DICED CUCUMBER

In blender, combine grape juice, grapes, and cucumber and blend until mixture is smooth. Pour into 1 tall glass.

EACH SERVING: ABOUT 205 CALORIES | 2 G PROTEIN | 50 G CARBOHYDRATE | 1 G TOTAL FAT (0 G SATURATED) | 0 MG CHOLESTEROL | 9 MG SODIUM

COFFEE-BANANA COOLER

Our winning blend of coffee yogurt and banana is especially smooth and creamy.

ACTIVE TIME: 5 MINUTES · **TOTAL TIME:** 5 MINUTES PLUS FREEZING

MAKES: 1¾ CUPS OR 1 SERVING

¼ CUP MILK

1 FROZEN BANANA, SLICED

1 CONTAINER (8 OUNCES) COFFEE YOGURT

In blender, combine milk, banana, and yogurt and blend until mixture is smooth and frothy. Pour into 1 tall glass.

EACH SERVING: ABOUT 356 CALORIES | 13 G PROTEIN | 66 G CARBOHYDRATE | 6 G TOTAL FAT (4 G SATURATED) | 23 MG CHOLESTEROL | 191 MG SODIUM

FROZEN FRUIT BOWL

This kid-friendly smoothie is a great way to get in those "two-to-four" servings of fruit. Use whatever combination of frozen fruit you have on hand. Kids might like this a bit sweeter, so add honey to taste.

ACTIVE TIME: 10 MINUTES · **TOTAL TIME:** 10 MINUTES

MAKES: 2 CUPS OR 1 SERVING

¾ CUP APPLE JUICE, CHILLED

¼ CUP MILK

½ CUP FROZEN STRAWBERRIES

½ CUP FROZEN SLICED PEACHES

¼ CUP FROZEN BLUEBERRIES

½ RIPE BANANA, SLICED

In blender, combine apple juice, milk, strawberries, peaches, blueberries, and banana and blend until mixture is smooth. Pour into 1 tall glass.

EACH SERVING: ABOUT 260 CALORIES | 4 G PROTEIN | 59 G CARBOHYDRATE | 3 G TOTAL FAT (1 G SATURATED) | 8 MG CHOLESTEROL | 41 MG SODIUM

SODA FOUNTAIN & COFFEE BAR FAVORITES

Banana-Split Shake (page 53)

DOUBLE-CHOCOLATE MALTED

Malt powder enriches the flavor of any milkshake. Look for it near the cocoa powder in your supermarket.

ACTIVE TIME: 5 MINUTES · **TOTAL TIME:** 5 MINUTES
MAKES: 3 CUPS OR 2 SERVINGS

4	SCOOPS CHOCOLATE ICE CREAM	3	TABLESPOONS CHOCOLATE SYRUP
1	CUP MILK	3	TABLESPOONS MALTED MILK POWDER

In blender, combine ice cream, milk, chocolate syrup, and malt powder and blend until mixture is smooth and frothy. Pour into 2 tall glasses.

EACH SERVING: ABOUT 348 CALORIES | 9 G PROTEIN | 47 G CARBOHYDRATE | 13 G TOTAL FAT (8 G SATURATED) | 44 MG CHOLESTEROL | 153 MG SODIUM

CLASSIC VANILLA MALTED

One taste and you'll see why this thick creamy treat has been a soda fountain favorite for years.

ACTIVE TIME: 5 MINUTES · **TOTAL TIME:** 5 MINUTES
MAKES: 2½ CUPS OR 2 SERVINGS

4	SCOOPS VANILLA ICE CREAM	2	TABLESPOONS MALTED MILK POWDER
1	CUP MILK	½	TEASPOON VANILLA EXTRACT

In blender, combine ice cream, milk, malt powder, and vanilla, and blend until mixture is smooth and frothy. Pour into 2 tall glasses.

EACH SERVING: ABOUT 258 CALORIES | 7 G PROTEIN | 25 G CARBOHYDRATE | 15 G TOTAL FAT (9 G SATURATED) | 53 MG CHOLESTEROL | 118 MG SODIUM

Double-Chocolate Malted

STRAWBERRY MALTED

If you like strawberries, you'll love this malted. You'll find strawberry-flavored syrup with the other syrups and drink mixes in your supermarket.

ACTIVE TIME : 5 MINUTES · **TOTAL TIME:** 5 MINUTES

MAKES: 2½ CUPS OR 2 SERVINGS

4	SCOOPS STRAWBERRY ICE CREAM	3	TABLESPOONS MALTED MILK POWDER
1	CUP MILK	2	TABLESPOONS STRAWBERRY-FLAVORED SYRUP

In blender, combine ice cream, milk, malt powder, and strawberry syrup and blend until mixture is smooth and frothy. Pour into 2 tall glasses.

EACH SERVING: ABOUT 306 CALORIES | 8 G PROTEIN | 44 G CARBOHYDRATE | 11 G TOTAL FAT (7 G SATURATED) | 39 MG CHOLESTEROL | 130 MG SODIUM

CLASSIC VANILLA MILKSHAKE

This is a truly singular sensation—pure vanilla all the way.

ACTIVE TIME: 5 MINUTES · **TOTAL TIME:** 5 MINUTES

MAKES: 2½ CUPS OR 2 SERVINGS

5   SCOOPS VANILLA ICE CREAM

1   CUP MILK

1   TEASPOON VANILLA EXTRACT

In blender, combine ice cream, milk, and vanilla, and blend until mixture is smooth and frothy. Pour into 2 tall glasses.

EACH SERVING: ABOUT 269 CALORIES | 6 G PROTEIN | 23 G CARBOHYDRATE | 16 G TOTAL FAT (10 G SATURATED) | 60 MG CHOLESTEROL | 97 MG SODIUM

CLASSIC CHOCOLATE MILKSHAKE

For those who delight in all things chocolate, make it a double helping—chocolate ice cream and chocolate syrup.

ACTIVE TIME: 5 MINUTES · **TOTAL TIME:** 5 MINUTES
MAKES: 2¼ CUPS OR 2 SERVINGS

---

4 SCOOPS VANILLA OR CHOCOLATE
   ICE CREAM

¾ CUP MILK

¼ CUP CHOCOLATE SYRUP

In blender, combine ice cream, milk, and chocolate syrup and blend until mixture is smooth and frothy. Pour into 2 tall glasses.

EACH SERVING: ABOUT 311 CALORIES | 6 G PROTEIN | 43 G CARBOHYDRATE | 13 G TOTAL FAT (8 G SATURATED) | 47 MG CHOLESTEROL | 102 MG SODIUM

MOCHA MALTED

The best of all possible worlds—coffee, chocolate, and malt all served up together in a tall glass.

ACTIVE TIME: 5 MINUTES · **TOTAL TIME:** 5 MINUTES
MAKES: 2 CUPS OR 2 SERVINGS

---

4 SCOOPS COFFEE ICE CREAM

1 CUP MILK

2 TABLESPOONS CHOCOLATE SYRUP

2 TABLESPOONS MALTED MILK POWDER

In blender, combine ice cream, milk, chocolate syrup, and malt powder and blend until mixture is smooth and frothy. Pour into 2 tall glasses.

EACH SERVING: ABOUT 297 CALORIES | 7 G PROTEIN | 39 G CARBOHYDRATE | 13 G TOTAL FAT (8 G SATURATED) | 43 MG CHOLESTEROL | 137 MG SODIUM

BANANA SHAKE

Rich, cool, and creamy.

ACTIVE TIME: 5 MINUTES · **TOTAL TIME:** 5 MINUTES

MAKES: 2½ CUPS OR 2 SERVINGS

---

1   CUP MILK

3   SCOOPS VANILLA ICE CREAM

1   BANANA, SLICED

In blender, combine milk, ice cream, and banana and blend until smooth and frothy. Pour into 2 tall glasses.

EACH SERVING: ABOUT 241 CALORIES | 6 G PROTEIN | 30 G CARBOHYDRATE | 12 G TOTAL FAT (7 G SATURATED) | 43 MG CHOLESTEROL | 83 MG SODIUM

COOKIES 'N' CREAM SHAKE

Kids will love their favorite combination mixed up in a glass.

ACTIVE TIME: 5 MINUTES · **TOTAL TIME:** 5 MINUTES

MAKES: 2 CUPS OR 2 SERVINGS

---

4   SCOOPS VANILLA ICE CREAM

4   CREAM-FILLED CHOCOLATE SANDWICH COOKIES, COARSELY CHOPPED

1   CUP MILK

In blender, combine ice cream, cookies, and milk and blend until mixture is smooth and frothy. Pour into 2 tall glasses.

EACH SERVING: ABOUT 332 CALORIES | 7 G PROTEIN | 35 G CARBOHYDRATE | 19 G TOTAL FAT (10 G SATURATED | 52 MG CHOLESTEROL | 236 MG SODIUM

DULCE DE LECHE SHAKE

Caramel (dulce de leche) ice cream tastes even richer and more flavorful when paired with caramel sauce.

ACTIVE TIME: 5 MINUTES · **TOTAL TIME:** 5 MINUTES
MAKES: 2½ CUPS OR 2 SERVINGS

1 CUP MILK

4 SCOOPS DULCE DE LECHE ICE CREAM

2 TABLESPOONS CARAMEL SAUCE

In blender, combine milk, ice cream, and caramel sauce and blend until mixture is smooth and frothy. Pour into 2 tall glasses.

EACH SERVING: ABOUT 430 CALORIES | 9 G PROTEIN | 49 G CARBOHYDRATE | 21 G TOTAL FAT (13 G SATURATED) | 117 MG CHOLESTEROL | 225 MG SODIUM

MOCHA FRAPPA CINNO

Our version of that famous coffee bar favorite. You can make it at home in a flash.

ACTIVE TIME: 10 MINUTES · **TOTAL TIME:** 10 MINUTES
MAKES 4 CUPS OR 4 SERVINGS

3 CUPS ICE CUBES

1 CUP STRONG BREWED COFFEE, CHILLED

¾ CUP MILK

⅓ CUP FUDGE SAUCE

2 TABLESPOONS SUGAR

In blender, combine ice, coffee, milk, fudge sauce, and sugar and blend until mixture is smooth and frothy. Pour into 4 glasses.

EACH SERVING: ABOUT 145 CALORIES | 3 G PROTEIN | 24 G CARBOHYDRATE | 4 G TOTAL FAT (2 G SATURATED) | 6 MG CHOLESTEROL | 63 G SODIUM

FROSTY CAPPUCCINO

Better than store-bought! A deceptively rich blender drink.

ACTIVE TIME: 5 MINUTES · TOTAL TIME: 5 MINUTES
MAKES: 1½ CUPS OR 2 SERVINGS

1 CUP LOW-FAT (1%) MILK	2 ICE CUBES
1 TABLESPOON CHOCOLATE SYRUP	SUGAR (OPTIONAL)
1 TEASPOON INSTANT ESPRESSO-COFFEE POWDER	⅛ TEASPOON GROUND CINNAMON

In blender, combine milk, chocolate syrup, espresso powder, and ice and blend until mixture is smooth and frothy. Add sugar to taste, if you like. Pour into 2 chilled glasses. Sprinkle with cinnamon for garnish.

EACH SERVING: ABOUT 75 CALORIES | 4 G PROTEIN | 12 G CARBOHYDRATE | 1 G TOTAL FAT (1 G SATURATED) | 5 MG CHOLESTEROL | 65 MG SODIUM

CREAMY ORANGE SHAKE

Brings back memories of a favorite ice cream treat.

ACTIVE TIME: 5 MINUTES · **TOTAL TIME:** 5 MINUTES
MAKES: 2½ CUPS OR 2 SERVINGS

---

5 SCOOPS VANILLA ICE CREAM

½ CUP ORANGE JUICE

⅓ CUP MILK

⅓ CUP FROZEN ORANGE JUICE CONCENTRATE

ORANGE PEEL (OPTIONAL GARNISH)

In blender, combine ice cream, orange juice, milk, and orange juice concentrate and blend until mixture is smooth and frothy. Pour into 2 tall glasses. Garnish with orange peel, if you like.

EACH SERVING: ABOUT 314 CALORIES | 5 G PROTEIN | 43 G CARBOHYDRATE | 14 G TOTAL FAT (8 G SATURATED) | 49 MG CHOLESTEROL | 59 MG SODIUM

KEY LIME SHAKE

Kick back your heels while you taste this refreshing shake, reminiscent of the laid-back Florida Keys.

ACTIVE TIME: 5 MINUTES · **TOTAL TIME:** 5 MINUTES
MAKES: 3 CUPS OR 2 SERVINGS

---

4 SCOOPS VANILLA ICE CREAM

1 CUP MILK

½ CUP FROZEN LIMEADE CONCENTRATE

1 TEASPOON FRESHLY GRATED LIME PEEL

In blender, combine ice cream, milk, limeade concentrate, and lime peel and blend until mixture is smooth and frothy. Pour into 2 tall glasses.

EACH SERVING: ABOUT 361 CALORIES | 6 G PROTEIN | 56 G CARBOHYDRATE | 14 G TOTAL FAT (9 G SATURATED) | 52 MG CHOLESTEROL | 89 MG SODIUM

Creamy Orange Shake

Root Beer Float

ROOT BEER FLOAT

This wonderful combination goes back to great grandma's day. In the 1960s, root beer floats were served in big mugs at A&W drive-ins by carhops and waitresses on roller skates.

ACTIVE TIME: 5 MINUTES · **TOTAL TIME:** 5 MINUTES
MAKES: 3 CUPS OR 2 SERVINGS

---

4   SCOOPS VANILLA ICE CREAM
1   CAN (12 OUNCES) ROOT BEER, CHILLED

1   In blender, combine 2 scoops ice cream and ¾ cup root beer and blend until mixture is smooth. Pour into 2 tall glasses.
2   Add a scoop of ice cream to each glass and fill with remaining root beer.

EACH SERVING: ABOUT 226 CALORIES | 2 G PROTEIN | 34 G CARBOHYDRATE | 10 G TOTAL FAT (6 G SATURATED) | 35 MG CHOLESTEROL | 54 MG SODIUM

PASSION FRUIT FLOAT

A sparkling taste of the tropics.

ACTIVE TIME: 5 MINUTES · **TOTAL TIME:** 5 MINUTES
MAKES: 2½ CUPS OR 2 SERVINGS

---

1   CAN (12 OUNCES) LEMON-LIME SODA, CHILLED
2   SCOOPS PASSION FRUIT SORBET
2   SCOOPS LEMON SORBET

1   In blender, combine ¾ cup soda and passion fruit sorbet and blend until mixture is smooth. Pour into 2 tall glasses.
2   Add a scoop of lemon sorbet to each glass. Fill with remaining soda.

EACH SERVING: ABOUT 202 CALORIES | 0 G PROTEIN | 46 G CARBOHYDRATE | 0 G TOTAL FAT (0 G SATURATED) | 0 MG CHOLESTEROL | 56 MG SODIUM

LEMON-BERRY SHAKE

The sweetness of the berries is balanced by the tang of fresh lemon. Served in a tall glass, this shake looks as pretty as a parfait.

ACTIVE TIME: 15 MINUTES · **TOTAL TIME:** 15 MINUTES

MAKES: 2⅔ CUPS OR 2 SERVINGS

1 CUP STRAWBERRIES, HULLED	2 TO 3 LEMONS
¼ CUP RASPBERRIES	4 SCOOPS VANILLA ICE CREAM
2 TABLESPOONS SUGAR	¾ CUP MILK

1 In blender, combine strawberries, raspberries, and sugar and blend until smooth. Pour into a glass; refrigerate.

2 From lemons, grate 1½ teaspoons peel and squeeze ⅓ cup juice.

3 In clean blender, combine lemon peel, lemon juice, ice cream, and milk and blend until mixture is smooth. Pour half of lemon mixture into 2 tall glasses. Top with half of berry puree. Repeat and gently stir until swirled.

EACH SERVING: ABOUT 293 CALORIES | 6 G PROTEIN | 41 G CARBOHYDRATE | 13 G TOTAL FAT (8 G SATURATED) | 47 MG CHOLESTEROL | 76 MG SODIUM

COCONUT-MANGO SHAKE

This icy combo of mango and coconut conjures up island breezes. Be sure to use light coconut milk.

ACTIVE TIME: 10 MINUTES · **TOTAL TIME:** 10 MINUTES

MAKES: 2½ CUPS OR 2 SERVINGS

1 LIME	1 CUP LIGHT COCONUT MILK
3 SCOOPS MANGO SORBET	¼ CUP WATER

1 From lime, grate 1½ teaspoons peel and squeeze 2 tablespoons juice.

2 In blender, combine lime peel, lime juice, mango sorbet, coconut milk, and water and blend until mixture is smooth and frothy. Pour shake into 2 tall glasses.

EACH SERVING: ABOUT 203 CALORIES | 2 G PROTEIN | 30 G CARBOHYDRATE | 10 G TOTAL FAT (6 G SATURATED) | 0 MG CHOLESTEROL | 15 MG SODIUM

BANANA-SPLIT SHAKE

We pulled out all the stops with this gooey concoction—whipped cream, chopped nuts, and maraschino cherries—then drizzled a little of the fudge sauce over the top.

ACTIVE TIME: 10 MINUTES · **TOTAL TIME:** 10 MINUTES
MAKES: 2½ CUPS OR 2 SERVINGS

4	TABLESPOONS FUDGE SAUCE	1	CUP MILK
1	BANANA, DICED		WHIPPED CREAM
4	MINI SCOOPS CHOCOLATE ICE CREAM	1	TABLESPOON CHOPPED WALNUTS OR PECANS
4	MINI SCOOPS STRAWBERRY ICE CREAM	2	MARASCHINO CHERRIES
4	SCOOPS VANILLA ICE CREAM		FUDGE SAUCE FOR GARNISH

1 In each of 2 tall glasses, place 2 tablespoons fudge sauce, half of the diced banana, 2 mini scoops chocolate ice cream, and 2 mini scoops strawberry ice cream.

2 In blender, combine vanilla ice cream and milk and blend until mixture is smooth. Add mixture to glasses; top each with whipped cream, walnuts, and cherry and drizzle with fudge sauce.

EACH SERVING: ABOUT 537 CALORIES | 11 G PROTEIN | 68 G CARBOHYDRATE | 26 G TOTAL FAT (14 G SATURATED) | 71 MG CHOLESTEROL | 288 MG SODIUM

PEACH MELBA SHAKE

Here's a great new take on a timeless classic. We took peaches, vanilla ice cream, and raspberry—the flavors that made peach melba such a popular dessert—and used them to make this sensational shake.

ACTIVE TIME: 5 MINUTES · **TOTAL TIME:** 5 MINUTES
MAKES: 2½ CUPS OR 2 SERVINGS

2   SCOOPS VANILLA ICE CREAM

3   CANNED PEACHES IN HEAVY SYRUP,
    DRAINED

1   DROP ALMOND EXTRACT

2   SCOOPS RASPBERRY SORBET

½   CUP CRANBERRY-RASPBERRY JUICE
    COCKTAIL, CHILLED

1 In blender, combine ice cream, peaches, and almond extract and blend until mixture is smooth. Pour into glass measure.
2 In same blender, combine sorbet and juice and blend until mixture is smooth. Pour half the peach and raspberry mixtures simultaneously into a glass so the shake is half peach- and half raspberry-colored. Repeat with the remaining mixtures in another glass.

EACH SERVING: ABOUT 279 CALORIES | 2 G PROTEIN | 60 G CARBOHYDRATE | 5 G TOTAL FAT (3 G SATURATED) | 18 MG CHOLESTEROL | 35 MG SODIUM

DEVILISH CHOCOLATE SHAKE

The name says it all—calling all chocoholics.

ACTIVE TIME: 5 MINUTES · **TOTAL TIME:** 5 MINUTES
MAKES: 2½ CUPS OR 2 SERVINGS

4   SCOOPS CHOCOLATE GELATO

1   CUP MILK

3   TABLESPOONS FUDGE SAUCE

In blender, combine gelato, milk, and fudge sauce and blend until mixture is smooth and frothy. Pour into 2 tall glasses.

EACH SERVING: ABOUT 412 CALORIES │ 10 G PROTEIN │ 58 G CARBOHYDRATE │ 16 G TOTAL FAT (9 G SATURATED) │ 100 MG CHOLESTEROL │ 245 MG SODIUM

COFFEE-DATE SHAKE

Dates add a natural sweetness to this shake. Die-hard coffee lovers can up the ante by substituting coffee ice cream for vanilla.

ACTIVE TIME: 10 MINUTES · **TOTAL TIME :** 10 MINUTES
MAKES: 2¼ CUPS OR 2 SERVINGS

¾   CUP MEDJOOL DATES, PITTED AND CHOPPED

½   CUP COLD BREWED COFFEE

¼   CUP MILK

3   SCOOPS VANILLA ICE CREAM

In blender, combine dates, coffee, and milk and blend until dates are pureed. Add ice cream and blend until mixture is smooth and frothy. Pour into 2 tall glasses.

EACH SERVING: ABOUT 316 CALORIES │ 4 G PROTEIN │ 61 G CARBOHYDRATE │ 9 G TOTAL FAT (5 G SATURATED) │ 30 MG CHOLESTEROL │ 41 MG SODIUM

Peppermint Stick Shake

PEPPERMINT STICK SHAKE

Use candy-cane sticks as stirrers. Kids will love it.

ACTIVE TIME: 10 MINUTES · **TOTAL TIME:** 10 MINUTES
MAKES: 2 CUPS OR 2 SERVINGS

8	ROUND HARD PEPPERMINT CANDIES	¾	CUP MILK
4	SCOOPS VANILLA ICE CREAM	¼	TEASPOON PEPPERMINT EXTRACT

In blender, blend candies until finely crushed. Add ice cream, milk, and peppermint extract and blend until mixture is smooth and frothy. Pour into 2 tall glasses.

EACH SERVING: ABOUT 302 CALORIES | 5 G PROTEIN | 42 G CARBOHYDRATE | 13 G TOTAL FAT (8 G SATURATED) | 47 MG CHOLESTEROL | 84 MG SODIUM

PEANUT-BUTTER-CUP SHAKE

Chocolate and peanut butter lovers will both be pleased with this candy-inspired confection.

ACTIVE TIME: 10 MINUTES · **TOTAL TIME:** 10 MINUTES
MAKES: 3 CUPS OR 2 SERVINGS

4	PEANUT-BUTTER-CUP CANDIES (.8 OUNCES EACH)	1	CUP MILK
4	SCOOPS CHOCOLATE ICE CREAM	¼	CUP PEANUT BUTTER

1 Chop peanut butter cups.
2 In blender, combine ice cream, milk, and peanut butter and blend until mixture is smooth. Add candies and blend until combined. Pour into 2 tall glasses.

EACH SERVING: ABOUT 685 CALORIES | 21 G PROTEIN | 54 G CARBOHYDRATE | 44 G TOTAL FAT (17 G SATURATED) | 45 MG CHOLESTEROL | 401 MG SODIUM

FIGGY FRAPPE

Depending on what part of the country you live in, a frappe can be a sundae, ice cream soda, or milkshake. But whatever your definition is, you'll savor this frosty, figgy one.

ACTIVE TIME: 5 MINUTES · **TOTAL TIME:** 5 MINUTES
MAKES: 2½ CUPS OR 2 SERVINGS

4 SCOOPS VANILLA ICE CREAM	4 DRIED FIGS, CHOPPED
1 CUP MILK	½ TEASPOON BRANDY EXTRACT

In blender, combine ice cream, milk, figs, and brandy extract and blend until mixture is smooth and frothy. Pour into 2 tall glasses.

EACH SERVING: ABOUT 325 CALORIES | 7 G PROTEIN | 45 G CARBOHYDRATE | 15 G TOTAL FAT (9 G SATURATED) | 52 MG CHOLESTEROL | 94 MG SODIUM

MAPLE PECAN FRAPPE

Maple syrup and pecans are a natural match. For best flavor, use grade B or C pure maple syrup—it has more maple flavor than grade A fancy.

ACTIVE TIME: 5 MINUTES · **TOTAL TIME:** 5 MINUTES
MAKES: 2 CUPS OR 2 SERVINGS

3 SCOOPS BUTTER-PECAN ICE CREAM
1 CUP MILK
¼ CUP PURE MAPLE SYRUP

In blender, combine ice cream, milk, and maple syrup and blend until mixture is smooth and frothy. Pour into 2 tall glasses.

EACH SERVING: ABOUT 300 CALORIES | 6 G PROTEIN | 44 G CARBOHYDRATE | 12 G TOTAL FAT (6 G SATURATED) | 35 MG CHOLESTEROL | 131 MG SODIUM

DOUBLE-GINGER FLOAT

Crystallized or candied ginger adds extra zing to this float.

ACTIVE TIME: 5 MINUTES · **TOTAL TIME:** 5 MINUTES
MAKES: 3 CUPS OR 2 SERVINGS

1 TABLESPOON CRYSTALLIZED GINGER	1 CAN (12 OUNCES) GINGER BEER OR GINGER ALE, CHILLED
4 SCOOPS VANILLA ICE CREAM	

1 In blender, process ginger until finely chopped. Add 2 scoops ice cream and ¾ cup ginger beer and blend until mixture is smooth. Pour into 2 tall glasses.

2 Add 1 scoop ice cream and half of remaining ginger beer to each glass.

EACH SERVING: ABOUT 228 CALORIES | 2 G PROTEIN | 34 G CARBOHYDRATE | 10 G TOTAL FAT (6 G SATURATED) | 35 MG CHOLESTEROL | 44 MG SODIUM

CHERRY-VANILLA FLOAT

This oldie-but-goodie is flavored with cherry cola.

ACTIVE TIME: 10 MINUTES · **TOTAL TIME:** 10 MINUTES
MAKES: 2½ CUPS OR 2 SERVINGS

2 SCOOPS VANILLA ICE CREAM	½ TEASPOON VANILLA EXTRACT
1 CAN (12 OUNCES) CHERRY-FLAVORED COLA, CHILLED	2 SCOOPS CHERRY ICE CREAM OR FROZEN YOGURT

1 In blender, combine vanilla ice cream, ¾ cup cola, and vanilla extract and blend until mixture is smooth. Pour into 2 tall glasses.

2 Add a scoop of cherry ice cream and remaining cola to each glass.

EACH SERVING: ABOUT 226 CALORIES | 2 G PROTEIN | 36 G CARBOHYDRATE | 9 G TOTAL FAT (5 G SATURATED) | 33 MG CHOLESTEROL | 57 MG SODIUM

FIZZES, SLUSHES & FROZEN COCKTAILS

Miami Mojito (page 76)

CLASSIC DAIQUIRI

The quintessential cocktail. You'll need 2 limes to get ¼ cup juice.

ACTIVE TIME: 5 MINUTES · **TOTAL TIME:** 5 MINUTES
MAKES: 3¾ CUPS OR 4 SERVINGS

---

4 CUPS ICE CUBES	¼ CUP FRESH LIME JUICE
¾ CUP LIGHT RUM	¼ CUP SIMPLE SYRUP, CHILLED (PAGE 87)

In blender, combine ice, rum, lime juice, and simple syrup and blend until mixture is smooth. Pour into 4 glasses.

EACH SERVING: ABOUT 146 CALORIES | 0 G PROTEIN | 13 G CARBOHYDRATE | 0 G TOTAL FAT (0 G SATURATED) | 0 MG CHOLESTEROL | 1 MG SODIUM

BANANA DAIQUIRI

Fruit makes a wonderful addition to daiquiris, marrying well with the rum. We used banana here, but peach, melon, strawberry, apricot, or mango would also be tasty.

ACTIVE TIME: 5 MINUTES · **TOTAL TIME:** 5 MINUTES
MAKES: 4 CUPS OR 4 SERVINGS

---

3 CUPS ICE CUBES	¼ CUP FRESH LIME JUICE
3 SMALL RIPE BANANAS, CUT INTO CHUNKS (ABOUT 2 CUPS)	2 TABLESPOONS SIMPLE SYRUP, CHILLED (PAGE 87)
¾ CUP LIGHT RUM	

In blender, combine ice, bananas, rum, lime juice, and simple syrup and blend until mixture is smooth. Pour into 4 glasses.

EACH SERVING: ABOUT 193 CALORIES | 1 G PROTEIN | 25 G CARBOHYDRATE | 1 G TOTAL FAT (0 G SATURATED) | 0 MG CHOLESTEROL | 1 MG SODIUM

STRAWBERRY MARGARITA

Pretty in pink—our fruity variation on the frosty margarita.

ACTIVE TIME: 10 MINUTES · **TOTAL TIME:** 10 MINUTES
MAKES: 5 CUPS OR 4 SERVINGS

---

4   CUPS ICE CUBES

1   PINT STRAWBERRIES, HULLED AND
    HALVED

½   CUP TEQUILA

⅓   CUP COINTREAU (ORANGE-FLAVORED
    LIQUEUR)

¼   CUP FRESH LIME JUICE

In blender, combine ice, berries, tequila, Cointreau, and lime juice and blend until mixture is smooth. Pour into 4 glasses.

EACH SERVING: ABOUT 149 CALORIES │ 1 G PROTEIN │ 12 G CARBOHYDRATE │ 0 G TOTAL FAT (0 G SATURATED) │ 0 MG CHOLESTEROL │ 1 MG SODIUM

FROSTY MARGARITA

Break out the salsa and chips.

ACTIVE TIME: 5 MINUTES · **TOTAL TIME:** 5 MINUTES
MAKES: 4 CUPS OR 4 SERVINGS

4   CUPS ICE CUBES

½   CUP TEQUILA

½   CUP COINTREAU (ORANGE-FLAVORED LIQUEUR)

¼   CUP FRESH LIME JUICE

In blender, combine ice, tequila, Cointreau, and lime juice and blend until mixture is smooth. Pour into 4 glasses.

EACH SERVING: ABOUT 154 CALORIES | 0 G PROTEIN | 10 G CARBOHYDRATE | 0 G TOTAL FAT (0 G SATURATED) | 0 MG CHOLESTEROL | 1 MG SODIUM

FROZEN MATADOR

You'll feel like you're south of the border without leaving home.

ACTIVE TIME: 5 MINUTES · **TOTAL TIME:** 5 MINUTES
MAKES: 4 CUPS OR 4 SERVINGS

4   CUPS ICE CUBES

¾   CUP TEQUILA

⅓   CUP PINEAPPLE JUICE, CHILLED

¼   CUP FRESH LIME JUICE

3   TABLESPOONS SIMPLE SYRUP, CHILLED (PAGE 87)

In blender, combine ice, tequila, juices, and simple syrup and blend until mixture is smooth. Pour into 4 glasses.

EACH SERVING: ABOUT 155 CALORIES | 0 G PROTEIN | 13 G CARBOHYDRATE | 0 G TOTAL FAT (0 G SATURATED) | 0 MG CHOLESTEROL | 1 MG SODIUM

Frosty Margarita

Frozen Piña Colada

FROZEN PIÑA COLADA

This sweet tropical drink was popular at the legendary Trader Vic's restaurant in New York City.

ACTIVE TIME: 5 MINUTES · TOTAL TIME: 5 MINUTES

MAKES: 4 CUPS OR 4 SERVINGS

4   CUPS ICE CUBES

¾   CUP PINEAPPLE JUICE, CHILLED

½   CUP GOLDEN RUM

½   CUP CREAM OF COCONUT

In blender, combine ice, juice, rum, and cream of coconut and blend until mixture is smooth and frothy. Pour into 4 glasses.

EACH SERVING: ABOUT 236 CALORIES | 0 G PROTEIN | 28 G CARBOHYDRATE | 5 G TOTAL FAT (4 G SATURATED) | 0 MG CHOLESTEROL | 16 MG SODIUM

ISLAND BREEZE

Kick back, sip, and imagine the cool refreshing embrace of the sea.

ACTIVE TIME: 5 MINUTES · TOTAL TIME: 5 MINUTES

MAKES: 4½ CUPS OR 4 SERVINGS

4   CUPS ICE CUBES

3   RIPE BANANAS, SLICED

¾   CUP DARK RUM

¾   CUP CREAM OF COCONUT

1   TABLESPOON FRESH LEMON JUICE

4   DASHES BITTERS

In blender, combine ice, bananas, rum, cream of coconut, lemon juice, and bitters and blend until mixture is smooth. Pour into 4 glasses.

EACH SERVING: ABOUT 397 CALORIES | 1 G PROTEIN | 54 G CARBOHYDRATE | 8 G TOTAL FAT (6 G SATURATED) | 0 MG CHOLESTEROL | 24 MG SODIUM

ZOMBIE

Remember those ceramic cups in the shape of carved heads? Here's the drink they were meant for. It's delicious and just a little decadent, as the name suggests.

ACTIVE TIME: 5 MINUTES · **TOTAL TIME:** 5 MINUTES

MAKES: 3 CUPS OR 4 SERVINGS

3 CUPS ICE CUBES	¼ CUP DARK RUM
½ CUP LIGHT RUM	¼ CUP APRICOT LIQUEUR
½ CUP PAPAYA NECTAR, CHILLED	3 TABLESPOONS FRESH LIME JUICE
	2 TABLESPOONS SIMPLE SYRUP, CHILLED (PAGE 87)

In blender, combine ice, light rum, papaya nectar, dark rum, liqueur, lime juice, and simple syrup and blend until the mixture is smooth. Pour into 4 tall glasses.

EACH SERVING: ABOUT 152 CALORIES | 0 G PROTEIN | 14 G CARBOHYDRATE | 0 G TOTAL FAT (0 G SATURATED) | 0 MG CHOLESTEROL | 3 MG SODIUM

BRANDY ALEXANDER

Dessert in a glass. To shave the chocolate easily, use a vegetable peeler.

ACTIVE TIME: 5 MINUTES · **TOTAL TIME:** 5 MINUTES
MAKES: 3 CUPS OR 4 SERVINGS

---

6   SCOOPS VANILLA ICE CREAM

½   CUP BRANDY

⅓   CUP DARK CRÈME DE CACAO

CHOCOLATE SHAVINGS

In blender, combine ice cream, brandy, and crème de cacao and blend until mixture is smooth and frothy. Pour into 4 stemmed glasses. Sprinkle with chocolate shavings.

EACH SERVING: ABOUT 255 CALORIES │ 2 G PROTEIN │ 19 G CARBOHYDRATE │ 8 G TOTAL FAT (5 G SATURATED) │ 26 MG CHOLESTEROL │ 24 MG SODIUM

RAMOS GIN FIZZ

This creamy concoction was named for Henry C. Ramos, who served it at his Imperial Cabinet saloon in New Orleans in the late 1880s. Ramos employed an entire staff just to shake the drinks, because it took at least five minutes to mix each one. Today all you need is your blender.

ACTIVE TIME: 10 MINUTES · **TOTAL TIME:** 10 MINUTES

MAKES: 4 CUPS OR 4 SERVINGS

3   CUPS ICE CUBES

¾   CUP GIN

¼   CUP HALF-AND-HALF OR LIGHT CREAM

¼   CUP SIMPLE SYRUP, CHILLED (PAGE 87)

2   TABLESPOONS FRESH LIME JUICE

2   TABLESPOONS FRESH LEMON JUICE

1   CUP CLUB SODA, CHILLED

1   In blender, combine ice cubes, gin, half-and-half, simple syrup, lime juice, and lemon juice and blend until mixture is smooth. Pour into 4 stemmed glasses.

2   Fill each glass with club soda and stir gently.

EACH SERVING: ABOUT 166 CALORIES | 1 G PROTEIN | 14 G CARBOHYDRATE | 2 G TOTAL FAT (1 G SATURATED) | 6 MG CHOLESTEROL | 19 MG SODIUM

SCORPION

Add a little sparkle to these citrusy cocktails. Rub an orange slice around the rim of each glass, then dip the moist rim into superfine sugar, turning glass to coat evenly.

ACTIVE TIME: 5 MINUTES · **TOTAL TIME:** 10 MINUTES
MAKES: 4 CUPS OR 4 SERVINGS

---

3   CUPS ICE CUBES

1   CUP FRESH ORANGE JUICE

½   CUP LIGHT OR GOLDEN RUM

⅓   CUP FRESH LEMON JUICE

¼   CUP BRANDY

¼   CUP SIMPLE SYRUP, CHILLED (PAGE 87)

In blender, combine ice, orange juice, rum, lemon juice, brandy, and simple syrup and blend until mixture is smooth. Pour into 4 glasses.

EACH SERVING: ABOUT 180 CALORIES │ 1 G PROTEIN │ 20 G CARBOHYDRATE │ 0 G TOTAL FAT (0 G SATURATED │ 0 MG CHOLESTEROL │ 1 MG SODIUM

RASPBERRY-LEMON SLUSH

A tasty something to sip for guests who don't want alcohol. Garnish each with a slice of lemon.

ACTIVE TIME: 5 MINUTES · **TOTAL TIME:** 5 MINUTES

MAKES: 4 CUPS OR 4 SERVINGS

---

1   PACKAGE (10 OUNCES) FROZEN RASPBERRIES IN SYRUP, THAWED

3   CUPS ICE CUBES

½   CUP FRESH LEMON JUICE

¼   CUP SIMPLE SYRUP, CHILLED (PAGE 87)

---

1   In blender, puree raspberries until smooth. Strain through a fine sieve; discard seeds.

2   In blender, combine raspberry puree, ice, lemon juice, and simple syrup and blend until mixture is smooth. Pour into 4 glasses.

EACH SERVING: ABOUT 171 CALORIES │ 1 G PROTEIN │ 43 G CARBOHYDRATE │ 0 G TOTAL FAT (0 G SATURATED) │ 0 MG CHOLESTEROL │ 21 MG SODIUM

MINT JULEP SLUSH

These taste so good you'll want to give a Kentucky Derby party.

ACTIVE TIME: 5 MINUTES · **TOTAL TIME:** 5 MINUTES

MAKES: 3½ CUPS OR 4 SERVINGS

---

8 LARGE SPRIGS FRESH MINT

4 CUPS ICE CUBES

¾ CUP BOURBON

¼ CUP SIMPLE SYRUP, CHILLED (PAGE 87)

---

1 Remove leaves from mint.

2 In blender, combine ice, bourbon, and simple syrup and blend until mixture is smooth. Add mint leaves; blend until leaves are coarsely chopped. Pour into 4 glasses.

EACH SERVING: ABOUT 152 CALORIES │ 0 G PROTEIN │ 12 G CARBOHYDRATE │ 0 G TOTAL FAT (0 G SATURATED) │ 0 MG CHOLESTEROL │ 1 MG SODIUM

COOL BLUE HAWAIIAN

This turquoise-blue drink is a favorite in the Hawaiian islands.

ACTIVE TIME: 5 MINUTES · **TOTAL TIME:** 5 MINUTES

MAKES: 4½ CUPS OR 4 SERVINGS

4	CUPS ICE CUBES	½	CUP CREAM OF COCONUT
1	CUP PINEAPPLE JUICE, CHILLED	4	PINEAPPLE SLICES
½	CUP BLUE CURAÇAO	4	MARASCHINO CHERRIES
½	CUP LIGHT RUM		

In blender, combine ice, pineapple juice, blue curaçao, rum, and cream of coconut and blend until mixture is smooth. Pour into 4 glasses. Garnish with pineapple slices and cherries.

EACH SERVING: ABOUT 366 CALORIES | 1 G PROTEIN | 51 G CARBOHYDRATE | 5 G TOTAL FAT (4 G SATURATED) | 0 MG CHOLESTEROL | 19 MG SODIUM

IRISH FROST

A mocha-flavored milkshake—for adults only.

ACTIVE TIME: 5 MINUTES · **TOTAL TIME:** 5 MINUTES
MAKES: 2¾ CUPS OR 5 SERVINGS

- 5 SCOOPS VANILLA ICE CREAM
- ¼ CUP BAILEY'S IRISH CREAM
- ¼ CUP WHITE CRÈME DE CACAO
- ¼ CUP KAHLÚA (COFFEE-FLAVORED LIQUEUR)
- ¼ CUP MILK
- 2 TABLESPOONS VODKA

In blender, combine ice cream, Bailey's, crème de cacao, Kahlúa, milk, and vodka and blend until mixture is smooth and frothy. Pour into 5 glasses.

EACH SERVING: ABOUT 221 CALORIES | 2 G PROTEIN | 20 G CARBOHYDRATE | 7 G TOTAL FAT (5 G SATURATED) | 21 MG CHOLESTEROL | 34 MG SODIUM

MIAMI MOJITO

This rum sparkler with its mint infusion is perfect for slow sipping while you watch a South Beach or, indeed, any sunset.

ACTIVE TIME: 10 MINUTES · **TOTAL TIME:** 10 MINUTES
MAKES: 6 CUPS OR 6 SERVINGS

- 8 LARGE SPRIGS FRESH MINT
- ½ CUP SUGAR
- ¼ CUP FRESH LIME JUICE
- 1½ TEASPOONS FRESHLY GRATED LIME PEEL
- 4 CUPS ICE CUBES
- 1 CUP GOLDEN RUM
- 3 CUPS CLUB SODA, CHILLED
- MINT SPRIGS FOR GARNISH

1 Remove leaves from mint sprigs. In blender, combine mint leaves, sugar, lime juice, and peel. Pulse until mint is chopped.
2 Fill pitcher with ice and add mint mixture. Pour in rum; stir. Fill with club soda. Pour into 6 glasses. Garnish with mint sprigs.

EACH SERVING: ABOUT 158 CALORIES | 0 G PROTEIN | 17 G CARBOHYDRATE | 0 G TOTAL FAT (0 G SATURATED) | 0 MG CHOLESTEROL | 26 MG SODIUM

BRANDIED EGGNOG

We used ice cream as the base for this eggnog, making it even richer and more festive—ideal for the holidays.

ACTIVE TIME: 5 MINUTES · **TOTAL TIME:** 5 MINUTES

MAKES: 2¼ CUPS OR 4 SERVINGS

---

5 SCOOPS FRENCH VANILLA ICE CREAM	2 TABLESPOONS GRAND MARNIER (ORANGE-FLAVORED LIQUEUR)
⅓ CUP BRANDY	¼ TEASPOON GRATED NUTMEG
¼ CUP MILK	

In blender, combine ice cream, brandy, milk, Grand Marnier, and ⅛ teaspoon nutmeg and blend until mixture is smooth and frothy. Pour into 4 glasses and sprinkle with remaining nutmeg.

EACH SERVING: ABOUT 179 CALORIES | 2 G PROTEIN | 13 G CARBOHYDRATE | 7 G TOTAL FAT (4 G SATURATED) | 36 MG CHOLESTEROL | 26 MG SODIUM

CREAMY GRASSHOPPER

This is an ultrarich frosty variation on the original. With a crisp cookie, it makes a great dessert.

ACTIVE TIME: 5 MINUTES · **TOTAL TIME:** 5 MINUTES

MAKES: 2¼ CUPS OR 4 SERVINGS

---

4 SCOOPS VANILLA ICE CREAM	⅓ CUP WHITE CRÈME DE CACAO
⅓ CUP GREEN CRÈME DE MENTHE	⅓ CUP MILK

In blender, combine ice cream, crème de menthe, crème de cacao, and milk and blend until mixture is smooth and frothy. Pour into 4 glasses.

EACH SERVING: ABOUT 254 CALORIES | 2 G PROTEIN | 27 G CARBOHYDRATE | 6 G TOTAL FAT (3 G SATURATED) | 20 MG CHOLESTEROL | 27 MG SODIUM

BROWN COW

We took the black-and-white milkshake—vanilla ice cream and chocolate syrup—and kicked it up a notch with a quick hit of Kahlúa (coffee-flavored liqueur).

ACTIVE TIME: 5 MINUTES · **TOTAL TIME:** 5 MINUTES
MAKES: 2⅔ CUPS OR 4 SERVINGS

4	SCOOPS VANILLA ICE CREAM	¼	CUP MILK
⅓	CUP KAHLÚA (COFFEE-FLAVORED LIQUEUR)	¼	CUP CHOCOLATE SYRUP

In blender, combine ice cream, Kahlúa, milk, and chocolate syrup and blend until mixture is smooth and frothy. Pour into 4 glasses.

EACH SERVING: ABOUT 196 CALORIES │ 2 G PROTEIN │ 26 G CARBOHYDRATE │ 6 G TOTAL FAT (3 G SATURATED) │ 20 MG CHOLESTEROL │ 42 MG SODIUM

SEA BREEZE

Originally made with gin, today's breezes are based on vodka. They taste best made with freshly squeezed grapefruit juice, either pink or white.

ACTIVE TIME: 5 MINUTES · **TOTAL TIME:** 5 MINUTES
MAKES: 3½ CUPS OR 4 SERVINGS

2	CUPS ICE CUBES	¾	CUP CRANBERRY JUICE, CHILLED
1	CUP GRAPEFRUIT JUICE, CHILLED	¾	CUP VODKA

In blender, combine ice, grapefruit juice, cranberry juice, and vodka and blend until mixture is smooth. Pour into 4 glasses.

EACH SERVING: ABOUT 147 CALORIES │ 0 G PROTEIN │ 13 G CARBOHYDRATE, │ 0 G TOTAL FAT (0 G SATURATED) │ 0 MG CHOLESTEROL │ 2 MG SODIUM

MOCHA MADNESS

Enjoy a luscious dessert, coffee, and after-dinner drink all in one glass. Serve it in cups and saucers with a coffee bean on top.

ACTIVE TIME: 5 MINUTES · TOTAL TIME: 5 MINUTES

MAKES: 2½ CUPS OR 4 SERVINGS

5   SCOOPS VANILLA ICE CREAM

½   CUP BREWED COFFEE, CHILLED

¼   CUP BRANDY

¼   CUP CRÈME DE CACAO

In blender, combine ice cream, coffee, brandy, and crème de cacao and blend until mixture is smooth. Pour into 4 glasses.

EACH SERVING: ABOUT 193 CALORIES | 1 G PROTEIN | 16 G CARBOHYDRATE | 6 G TOTAL FAT (4 G SATURATED) | 22 MG CHOLESTEROL | 20 MG SODIUM

ALMOND CREAM

Top with some toasted slivered almonds.

ACTIVE TIME: 5 MINUTES · TOTAL TIME: 5 MINUTES

MAKES: 2½ CUPS OR 4 SERVINGS

4   SCOOPS VANILLA ICE CREAM

¼   CUP AMARETTO (ALMOND-FLAVORED LIQUEUR)

¼   CUP KAHLÚA (COFFEE-FLAVORED LIQUEUR)

¼   CUP MILK

In blender, combine ice cream, amaretto, Kahlúa, and milk and blend until mixture is smooth and frothy. Pour into 4 glasses.

EACH SERVING: ABOUT 191 CALORIES | 2 G PROTEIN | 20 G CARBOHYDRATE | 6 G TOTAL FAT (3 G SATURATED) | 20 MG CHOLESTEROL | 25 MG SODIUM

FROZEN WATERMELON SLUSH

A refreshing, colorful drink for those dog days of summer. If you have extra watermelon, you can freeze it for more slushes.

ACTIVE TIME: 5 MINUTES · **TOTAL TIME:** 5 MINUTES
MAKES: 3½ CUPS OR 4 SERVINGS

3	CUPS CUBED SEEDLESS WATERMELON	¼	CUP PINEAPPLE JUICE, CHILLED
1	CUP FROZEN STRAWBERRIES	2	TABLESPOONS FRESH LIME JUICE
2	SCOOPS LEMON SORBET		

In blender, combine watermelon, strawberries, sorbet, pineapple juice, and lime juice and blend until mixture is smooth. Pour into 4 glasses.

EACH SERVING: ABOUT 87 CALORIES | 1 G PROTEIN | 22 G CARBOHYDRATE | 0 G TOTAL FAT (0 G SATURATED) | 0 MG CHOLESTEROL | 7 MG SODIUM

RED WINE SANGRIA SLUSH

A real crowd pleaser. For a party, triple or quadruple the ingredients and pour into a chilled pitcher.

ACTIVE TIME: 5 MINUTES · **TOTAL TIME:** 5 MINUTES
MAKES: 3 CUPS OR 4 SERVINGS

2	CUPS ICE CUBES	½	CUP FROZEN ORANGE JUICE CONCENTRATE
¾	CUP FROZEN PITTED SWEET CHERRIES		
1	CUP FRUITY RED WINE, CHILLED	1	TABLESPOON FRESH LIME JUICE

In blender, combine ice, cherries, wine, orange juice concentrate, and lime juice and blend until mixture is smooth. Pour into 4 glasses.

EACH SERVING: ABOUT 142 CALORIES | 2 G PROTEIN | 26 G CARBOHYDRATE | 0 G TOTAL FAT (0 G SATURATED) | 0 MG CHOLESTEROL | 5 MG SODIUM

Frozen Watermelon Slush

Frozen Iced Tea

FROZEN ICED TEA

Lemon or passion fruit sorbet would also be delicious in this drink.

ACTIVE TIME: 5 MINUTES · **TOTAL TIME:** 5 MINUTES
MAKES: 3½ CUPS OR 4 SERVINGS

---

4   SCOOPS ORANGE SORBET

2   CUPS STRONG BREWED BLACK TEA, AT
    ROOM TEMPERATURE

In blender, combine sorbet and tea and blend until mixture is smooth. Pour into 4 glasses.

EACH SERVING: ABOUT 61 CALORIES | 0 G PROTEIN | 15 G CARBOHYDRATE | 0 G TOTAL FAT (0 G SATURATED) | 0 MG CHOLESTEROL | 11 MG SODIUM

FROZEN WHISKEY SOUR

A cool twist on the straight-up whiskey sour.

ACTIVE TIME: 5 MINUTES · **TOTAL TIME:** 5 MINUTES
MAKES: 3½ CUPS OR 4 SERVINGS

---

4   CUPS ICE CUBES   ¾   CUP WHISKEY

1   CAN (6 OUNCES) FROZEN LEMONADE
    CONCENTRATE

In blender, combine ice, lemonade concentrate, and whiskey and blend until mixture is smooth. Pour into 4 glasses.

EACH SERVING: ABOUT 209 CALORIES | 0 G PROTEIN | 26 G CARBOHYDRATE | 0 G TOTAL FAT (0 G SATURATED) | 0 MG CHOLESTEROL | 3 MG SODIUM

FROZEN VIRGIN MARY

To make them more festive, garnish each drink with a lemon wedge.
Then add a celery stalk, which can double as a stirrer.

ACTIVE TIME: 5 MINUTES · **TOTAL TIME:** 5 MINUTES

MAKES: 4 CUPS OR 4 SERVINGS

3   CUPS ICE CUBES

2   CUPS VEGETABLE JUICE, CHILLED

3   TABLESPOONS FRESH LEMON JUICE

1   TO 2 TEASPOONS PREPARED WHITE
    HORSERADISH

1   TEASPOON WORCESTERSHIRE SAUCE

¼   TO ½ TEASPOON HOT PEPPER SAUCE

⅛   TEASPOON FRESHLY GROUND
    BLACK PEPPER

In blender, combine ice, vegetable juice, lemon juice, horseradish,
Worcestershire, hot pepper sauce, and black pepper and blend until
smooth. Pour into 4 tall glasses.

EACH SERVING: ABOUT 30 CALORIES | 1 G PROTEIN | 6 G CARBOHYDRATE | 0 G TOTAL FAT
(0 G SATURATED) | 0 MG CHOLESTEROL | 330 MG SODIUM

CLASSIC BELLINI

As classy as the original created at Harry's Bar in Venice.

ACTIVE TIME: 5 MINUTES · **TOTAL TIME:** 5 MINUTES

MAKES: 4 CUPS OR 4 SERVINGS

---

2   RIPE PEACHES, PITTED AND DICED

2   TEASPOONS FRESH LEMON JUICE

2   TEASPOONS SIMPLE SYRUP, CHILLED (PAGE 87)

1   BOTTLE (750 ML) BRUT CHAMPAGNE OR SPARKLING WINE, CHILLED

In blender, combine peaches, lemon juice, and simple syrup and blend until mixture is smooth. Pour into 4 champagne flutes, then fill with champagne.

EACH SERVING: ABOUT 162 CALORIES | 1 G PROTEIN | 12 G CARBOHYDRATE | 0 G TOTAL FAT (0 G SATURATED) | 0 MG CHOLESTEROL | 0 MG SODIUM

BABY BELLINI

Our non-alcoholic Bellini, made with sparkling apple juice, stays as bubbly as the original.

ACTIVE TIME: 5 MINUTES · **TOTAL TIME:** 5 MINUTES

MAKES: 4 CUPS OR 4 SERVINGS

---

2   RIPE PEACHES, PITTED AND DICED

2   TEASPOONS FRESH LEMON JUICE

2   TEASPOONS SIMPLE SYRUP, CHILLED (PAGE 87)

1   BOTTLE (750 ML) SPARKLING APPLE JUICE, CHILLED

In blender, combine peaches, lemon juice, and simple syrup and blend until mixture is smooth. Pour into 4 champagne flutes, then fill with sparkling apple juice.

EACH SERVING: ABOUT 122 CALORIES | 0 G PROTEIN | 30 G CARBOHYDRATE | 0 G TOTAL FAT (0 G SATURATED) | 0 MG CHOLESTEROL | 6 MG SODIUM

SIMPLE SYRUP

This sugar syrup is great in cold drinks, such as iced tea, because it dissolves instantly. It also lets you control the exact amount of sweetness when making drinks, because you can add it just a little at a time, as you taste. Keep some on hand in the refrigerator—it will last for up to a month.

ACTIVE TIME: 5 MINUTES · **TOTAL TIME:** 15 MINUTES
MAKES: 2 CUPS

---

2 CUPS SUGAR

1 CUP WATER

In a small saucepan, combine sugar and water. Bring to a boil. Reduce heat to low; simmer 10 minutes. Cool and refrigerate until chilled.

PER TEASPOON: ABOUT 16 CALORIES | 0 G PROTEIN | 2 G CARBOHYDRATE | 0 G TOTAL FAT (0 G SATURATED) | 0 MG CHOLESTEROL | 0 MG SODIUM

SENSATIONAL SOUPS

Cold Avocado Soup (page 119)

BUTTERNUT-APPLE SOUP

Elegant and autumnal, this silky-smooth golden soup is the perfect beginning for a holiday meal.

ACTIVE TIME: 15 MINUTES · **TOTAL TIME:** 55 TO 60 MINUTES

MAKES: ABOUT 9 CUPS OR 8 FIRST-COURSE SERVINGS

2 TABLESPOONS VEGETABLE OIL	1½ CUPS WATER
1 SMALL ONION, CHOPPED	1 TEASPOON FRESH THYME OR ¼ TEASPOON DRIED THYME
2 MEDIUM BUTTERNUT SQUASH (1¾ POUNDS EACH), PEELED, SEEDED, AND CUT INTO ¾-INCH PIECES	1 TEASPOON SALT
¾ POUND GOLDEN DELICIOUS APPLES (2 MEDIUM), PEELED, CORED, AND COARSELY CHOPPED	⅛ TEASPOON COARSELY GROUND BLACK PEPPER
1 CAN (14 ½ OUNCES) VEGETABLE BROTH	1 CUP HALF-AND-HALF OR LIGHT CREAM

1 In 4-quart saucepan, heat oil over medium heat. Add onion and cook until tender and golden, about 10 minutes. Stir in the squash, apples, vegetable broth, water, thyme, salt, and pepper; heat to boiling over high heat. Reduce heat; cover saucepan and simmer, stirring often, until squash is very tender, 20 to 25 minutes.

2 Spoon one-third of squash mixture into blender; cover, with center part of cover removed to let steam escape, and puree until smooth. Pour pureed soup into large bowl after each batch. Repeat with remaining mixture.

3 Return puree to saucepan; stir in half-and-half. Heat through over medium heat, stirring occasionally (do not boil).

EACH SERVING: ABOUT 175 CALORIES | 3 G PROTEIN | 28 G CARBOHYDRATE | 7 MG TOTAL FAT (3 MG SATURATED) | 11 MG CHOLESTEROL | 525 MG SODIUM

CARROT AND DILL SOUP

Combine sweet carrots with fresh orange, dill, and a touch of milk for a satisfyingly creamy soup without the cream.

ACTIVE TIME: 25 MINUTES · **TOTAL TIME:** 1 HOUR, 10 MINUTES

MAKES: ABOUT 10½ CUPS OR 10 FIRST-COURSE SERVINGS

1	TABLESPOON OLIVE OIL	¾	TEASPOON SALT
1	LARGE ONION, CHOPPED	¼	TEASPOON COARSELY GROUND BLACK PEPPER
1	MEDIUM STALK CELERY, CHOPPED		
2	LARGE ORANGES	4	CUPS WATER
2	BAGS (16 OUNCES EACH) CARROTS, CHOPPED	1	CUP MILK
		¼	CUP CHOPPED FRESH DILL
1	CAN (14½ OUNCES) CHICKEN BROTH		DILL SPRIGS FOR GARNISH
1	TABLESPOON SUGAR		

1 In 5-quart Dutch oven, heat olive oil over medium-high heat. Add onion and celery and cook, stirring occasionally, until tender and golden, about 15 minutes.

2 Meanwhile, with vegetable peeler, from 1 orange, remove 4 strips of peel (3" by 1" each) and squeeze 1 cup juice from both oranges.

3 Add orange-peel strips to Dutch oven and cook 2 minutes longer, stirring. Add orange juice, carrots, chicken broth, sugar, salt, pepper, and water; heat to boiling over high heat. Reduce heat to low; cover and simmer 25 minutes or until carrots are very tender.

4 Remove orange-peel strips from soup. In blender, with center part of cover removed to allow steam to escape, blend soup in small batches until pureed and smooth. Pour pureed soup into large bowl after each batch.

5 Return puree to Dutch oven; stir in milk and chopped dill; heat just to simmering over medium heat. Garnish each serving with a dill sprig.

EACH SERVING: ABOUT 95 CALORIES | 3 G PROTEIN | 16 G CARBOHYDRATE | 3 G TOTAL FAT (1 G SATURATED | 3 MG CHOLESTEROL | 335 MG SODIUM

CURRIED CARROT SOUP

Use a good-quality mild Madras-style curry powder for spice without heat. Briefly sautéing the curry powder releases all its complex flavors.

ACTIVE TIME: 25 MINUTES · **TOTAL TIME:** 1 HOUR, 10 MINUTES

MAKES: ABOUT 13 CUPS OR 12 FIRST-COURSE SERVINGS

2   TABLESPOONS OLIVE OIL

1   JUMBO ONION (1 POUND), CHOPPED

4   TEASPOONS CURRY POWDER

1   TABLESPOON GRATED, PEELED FRESH GINGER

3   BAGS (16 OUNCES EACH) CARROTS, PEELED AND COARSELY CHOPPED

2   CANS (14½ OUNCES EACH) CHICKEN BROTH

6   CUPS WATER

1½ TEASPOONS SALT

1   CUP HALF-AND-HALF OR LIGHT CREAM

1   In 5-quart Dutch oven, heat oil over medium heat. Add onion; cook until tender and golden, 10 to 15 minutes.

2   Add curry powder and ginger; cook, stirring constantly, 1 minute. Add carrots, broth, 2 cups water, and salt; heat to boiling. Reduce heat; cover and simmer until carrots are very tender, about 20 minutes. Cool slightly.

3   In blender, with center part of cover removed to allow steam to escape, puree one-fourth of carrot mixture until smooth. Pour pureed soup into large bowl after each batch. Repeat with remaining mixture.

4   Return puree to Dutch oven; stir in half-and-half and remaining 4 cups water. Heat through over medium heat, stirring frequently (do not boil).

EACH SERVING: ABOUT 115 CALORIES | 3 G PROTEIN | 15 G CARBOHYDRATE | 5 G TOTAL FAT (2 G SATURATED) | 7 MG CHOLESTEROL | 621 MG SODIUM

YELLOW SQUASH AND BASIL SOUP

Float a bright edible flower, such as a pansy or nasturtium, on top of the soup—or place it on the rim of the bowl.

ACTIVE TIME: 10 MINUTES · **TOTAL TIME:** ABOUT 40 MINUTES

MAKES: ABOUT 8 CUPS OR 10 FIRST-COURSE SERVINGS

---

4 TABLESPOONS BUTTER OR MARGARINE

1 MEDIUM ONION, FINELY CHOPPED

4 SMALL YELLOW SQUASHES (ABOUT 8 OUNCES EACH), SLICED

3 MEDIUM CARROTS, PEELED AND SLICED

1 CAN (14½ OUNCES) CHICKEN BROTH

1½ CUPS WATER

½ CUP HALF-AND-HALF OR LIGHT CREAM

1¼ TEASPOONS SALT

¼ TEASPOON COARSELY GROUND BLACK PEPPER

1 CUP LOOSELY PACKED FRESH BASIL LEAVES, CHOPPED

1 In 4-quart saucepan, melt butter or margarine over medium heat. Add onion and cook about 8 minutes or until onion is tender but not brown, stirring frequently.

2 Add squash and carrot slices and stir vegetables to coat with onion mixture. Add chicken broth and water; heat to boiling over high heat. Reduce heat to low; cover and simmer 20 minutes or until vegetables are tender.

3 In blender at low speed, with center part of cover removed to allow steam to escape, blend soup in small batches until pureed. Pour pureed soup into large bowl after each batch.

4 Return puree to saucepan; stir in half-and-half, salt, and pepper, and heat through. Stir in chopped basil just before serving.

EACH SERVING: ABOUT 55 CALORIES | 3 G PROTEIN | 9 G CARBOHYDRATE | 2 G TOTAL FAT (1 G SATURATED) | 4 MG CHOLESTEROL | 845 MG SODIUM

CREAM OF ASPARAGUS SOUP

For the most flavor, choose the thickest asparagus you can find for this creamy soup. If you wish, garnish each serving with a sprinkling of chopped fresh chives, tarragon, or parsley.

ACTIVE TIME: 10 MINUTES · **TOTAL TIME:** 35 TO 40 MINUTES

MAKES: ABOUT 5 CUPS OR 4 FIRST-COURSE SERVINGS

2 TABLESPOONS BUTTER OR MARGARINE

1 MEDIUM ONION, CHOPPED

12 OUNCES ASPARAGUS, TRIMMED AND CUT INTO 1-INCH PIECES (3 CUPS)

3 TABLESPOONS ALL-PURPOSE FLOUR

¼ TEASPOON SALT

⅛ TEASPOON GROUND BLACK PEPPER

1 CAN (14½ OUNCES) CHICKEN OR VEGETABLE BROTH

1 CUP HALF-AND-HALF OR LIGHT CREAM

1 In 3-quart saucepan, melt butter over medium heat; add onion and cook, stirring frequently, until tender and golden, about 10 minutes. Add asparagus; cook 1 minute.

2 Stir in flour, salt, and pepper until blended. Gradually stir in broth; heat to boiling, stirring constantly. Reduce heat; cover and simmer until asparagus is tender, 5 to 10 minutes.

3 In blender, with center part of cover removed to allow steam to escape, puree half of mixture until smooth. Pour puree into bowl. Repeat with remaining mixture.

4 Return puree to saucepan; stir in half-and-half. Heat through (do not boil). Serve soup hot, or cover and refrigerate to serve chilled later. If chilled soup is too thick, stir in some milk.

EACH SERVING: ABOUT 194 CALORIES | 6 G PROTEIN | 14 G CARBOHYDRATE | 14 G TOTAL FAT (8 G SATURATED) | 38 MG CHOLESTEROL | 657 MG SODIUM

CREAM OF SPINACH SOUP

MAKES: ABOUT 3⅔ CUPS OR 4 FIRST-COURSE SERVINGS

Prepare as directed but substitute 1 bag (10 ounces) fresh spinach, **tough stems trimmed**, for asparagus and omit the 5 to 10 minutes of cooking time in step 2.

QUICK CREAM OF BROCCOLI SOUP

Frozen vegetables are picked and processed so quickly they often retain more nutrients than fresh. Here, broccoli and our other variations easily transform into satisfying soups.

ACTIVE TIME: 5 MINUTES · **TOTAL TIME:** 25 MINUTES

MAKES: ABOUT 3¾ CUPS OR 4 FIRST-COURSE SERVINGS

1	TABLESPOON BUTTER OR MARGARINE	⅛	TEASPOON GROUND BLACK PEPPER
1	MEDIUM ONION, CHOPPED		PINCH GROUND NUTMEG
1	PACKAGE (10 OUNCES) FROZEN CHOPPED BROCCOLI		PINCH GROUND RED PEPPER (CAYENNE; OPTIONAL)
1	CAN (14½ OUNCES) CHICKEN BROTH	1½	CUPS MILK
¼	TEASPOON DRIED THYME	2	TEASPOONS FRESH LEMON JUICE
⅛	TEASPOON SALT		

1 In 3-quart saucepan, melt butter over medium heat. Add onion and cook, stirring occasionally, until tender, about 5 minutes. Add broccoli, broth, thyme, salt, pepper, nutmeg, and ground red pepper, if using; heat to boiling over high heat. Reduce heat and simmer 10 minutes.

2 In blender, with center part of cover removed to allow steam to escape, puree half of mixture until smooth. Pour pureed soup into large bowl after each batch. Repeat with remaining mixture.

3 Return puree to saucepan; stir in milk. Heat through, stirring often (do not boil). Remove from heat and stir in lemon juice.

EACH SERVING: ABOUT 130 CALORIES | 6 G PROTEIN | 12 G CARBOHYDRATE | 7 G TOTAL FAT (4 G SATURATED) | 21 MG CHOLESTEROL | 594 MG SODIUM

QUICK CREAM OF PEA SOUP

Prepare as directed but substitute **1 package (10 ounces) frozen peas** for broccoli; if you like, add ¼ teaspoon **dried mint leaves** with broth.

QUICK CREAM OF ASPARAGUS SOUP

Prepare as directed but substitute **1 package (10 ounces) frozen asparagus** for broccoli; if you like, add **¼ teaspoon dried tarragon** with broth.

QUICK CREAM OF SQUASH SOUP

Prepare as directed but substitute **1 package (10 ounces) frozen cooked winter squash** for broccoli; if you like, add **¼ teaspoon pumpkin-pie spice** after cooking onion and cook 30 seconds before adding broth.

QUICK CREAM OF CORN SOUP

Prepare as directed but substitute **1 package (10 ounces) frozen whole-kernel corn** for broccoli; if you like, add **¾ teaspoon chili powder** after cooking onion and cook 30 seconds before adding broth.

QUICK CREAM OF CAULIFLOWER SOUP

Prepare as directed but substitute **1 package (10 ounces) frozen cauliflower flowerets** for broccoli; if you like, add **½ teaspoon curry powder** after cooking onion and cook 30 seconds before adding broth. Garnish with chopped fresh apple.

ASIAN-STYLE CORN CHOWDER

Andrea Spencer, sister-in-law of GH Food Appliances Director Sharon Franke, began making this spicy corn soup about ten years ago, adapting it from Ken Hom's *East Meets West Cuisine*.

ACTIVE TIME: 20 MINUTES · **TOTAL TIME:** ABOUT 35 MINUTES
MAKES: ABOUT 9½ CUPS OR 10 FIRST-COURSE SERVINGS

2 TABLESPOONS BUTTER OR MARGARINE

2 TABLESPOONS MINCED, PEELED FRESH GINGER

2 MEDIUM SHALLOTS, MINCED

2 MEDIUM GARLIC CLOVES, MINCED

1 MEDIUM ONION, DICED

1 STALK (12 INCHES LONG) FRESH LEMONGRASS, LIGHTLY POUNDED AND THEN CUT INTO 4-INCH-LONG PIECES OR 3 STRIPS LEMON PEEL (3" BY 1" EACH)

2 CANS (14½ OUNCES EACH) CHICKEN BROTH

1 BAG (20 OUNCES) FROZEN WHOLE-KERNEL CORN, THAWED

1½ TEASPOONS SUGAR

½ TEASPOON SALT

2 CUPS WATER

½ CUP HALF-AND-HALF OR LIGHT CREAM

CHOPPED FRESH CILANTRO LEAVES FOR GARNISH

CHILI PASTE* (OPTIONAL)

1 In 6-quart saucepot, melt butter or margarine over medium heat. Add ginger, shallots, garlic, onion, and lemongrass or lemon peel and cook until golden, about 8 minutes.

2 Add chicken broth, corn, sugar, salt, and water; heat to boiling over high heat. Reduce heat to low; cover and simmer 5 minutes. Discard lemongrass or lemon peel. Remove 2 cups soup; reserve.

3 In blender at low speed, with center part of cover removed to allow steam to escape, blend soup remaining in saucepot in small batches until very smooth. Pour pureed soup into large bowl after each batch.

4 Return blended soup and reserved soup to saucepot; stir in half-and-half. Heat soup over medium heat until hot, stirring occasionally. Serve soup with cilantro and chili paste if you like.

*TIP Chili paste is a spicy-hot condiment that can be found in Asian markets or in the ethnic food section of some supermarkets.

EACH SERVING: ABOUT 110 CALORIES | 4 G PROTEIN | 16 G CARBOHYDRATE | 4 G TOTAL FAT (1 G SATURATED) | 4 MG CHOLESTEROL | 410 MG SODIUM

WINTER VEGETABLE SOUP

An elegant pureed soup that's perfect as a company first course or, for a family dinner, just add salad, bread, and cheese.

ACTIVE TIME: 20 MINUTES · **TOTAL TIME:** 50 MINUTES

MAKES: ABOUT 10 CUPS OR 8 FIRST-COURSE SERVINGS

---

1 TABLESPOON VEGETABLE OIL

1 MEDIUM ONION, FINELY CHOPPED

1 GARLIC CLOVE, MINCED

1 BAG (16 OUNCES) CARROTS, SLICED

1 SMALL FENNEL BULB, TRIMMED AND DICED

2 CANS (14½ OUNCES EACH) CHICKEN OR VEGETABLE BROTH

¼ TEASPOON SALT, OR TO TASTE

¼ TEASPOON COARSELY GROUND BLACK PEPPER

3 CUPS WATER

3 MEDIUM ALL-PURPOSE POTATOES (ABOUT 1 POUND), PEELED AND EACH CUT INTO QUARTERS

½ CUP HALF-AND-HALF OR LIGHT CREAM (OPTIONAL)

DILL SPRIGS FOR GARNISH

---

1 In 5-quart saucepot, heat oil over medium heat. Add onion and garlic and cook 10 minutes or until tender, stirring occasionally. Stir in carrots, fennel, broth, salt, pepper, and water. Heat to boiling over high heat. Reduce heat to low; cover and simmer 10 minutes. Add potatoes and simmer 20 minutes longer or until vegetables are very tender.

2 In blender at low speed, with center part of cover removed to allow steam to escape, blend vegetable mixture in small batches until smooth; pour pureed soup into large bowl after each batch.

3 Return puree to saucepot; add half-and-half or light cream, if desired; heat through. Garnish each serving with a dill sprig.

EACH SERVING WITHOUT CREAM: ABOUT 100 CALORIES | 4 G PROTEIN | 16 G CARBOHYDRATE 3 G TOTAL FAT (0 G SATURATED) | 0 MG CHOLESTEROL | 420 MG SODIUM

GAZPACHO WITH CILANTRO CREAM

Recipes for this chilled Spanish soup abound—ours is topped with a dollop of cilantro-spiked sour cream.

ACTIVE TIME: 30 MINUTES · **TOTAL TIME:** 30 MINUTES PLUS CHILLING

MAKES: ABOUT 5 CUPS OR 4 FIRST-COURSE SERVINGS

2	MEDIUM CUCUMBERS (8 OUNCES EACH), PEELED	2	TABLESPOONS EXTRA VIRGIN OLIVE OIL
1	YELLOW PEPPER	¾	PLUS ⅛ TEASPOON SALT
¼	SMALL RED ONION	¼	CUP REDUCED-FAT SOUR CREAM OR PLAIN LOW-FAT YOGURT
2	POUNDS RIPE TOMATOES (5 MEDIUM), PEELED, SEEDED, AND CHOPPED	1	TABLESPOON MILK
½	TO 1 SMALL JALAPEÑO CHILE, SEEDED	4	TEASPOONS CHOPPED FRESH CILANTRO
3	TABLESPOONS FRESH LIME JUICE		

1 Chop half of 1 cucumber, half of yellow pepper, and all of onion into ¼-inch pieces; set aside. Cut remaining cucumbers and yellow pepper into large pieces.

2 In blender, combine large pieces of cucumber and yellow pepper, tomatoes, jalapeño, lime juice, oil, and ¾ teaspoon salt and blend until smooth. Pour puree into bowl; add cut-up cucumber, yellow pepper, and onion. Cover and refrigerate until well chilled, at least 6 hours or up to overnight.

3 Prepare cilantro cream: In small bowl, stir sour cream, milk, cilantro, and remaining ⅛ teaspoon salt until smooth. Cover and refrigerate.

4 To serve, top soup with dollops of cilantro cream.

EACH SERVING: ABOUT 156 CALORIES | 4 G PROTEIN | 17 G CARBOHYDRATE | 10 G TOTAL FAT (2 G SATURATED) | 6 MG CHOLESTEROL | 545 MG SODIUM

SHRIMP BISQUE

Bisque doesn't get any tastier than this—making a broth from the shrimp shells doubles the classic shrimp flavor.

ACTIVE TIME: 30 MINUTES · **TOTAL TIME:** 1 HOUR, 40 MINUTES

MAKES: ABOUT 10 CUPS OR 10 FIRST-COURSE SERVINGS

---

1   POUND MEDIUM SHRIMP

3   TABLESPOONS BUTTER OR MARGARINE

2   CANS (14½ OUNCES EACH), REDUCED-SODIUM CHICKEN BROTH

1   CUP DRY WHITE WINE

½   CUP WATER

2   MEDIUM CARROTS, CHOPPED

2   MEDIUM STALKS CELERY, CHOPPED

1   LARGE ONION, CHOPPED

2   TABLESPOONS REGULAR LONG-GRAIN RICE

1¼ TEASPOONS SALT

⅛   TO ¼ TEASPOON GROUND RED PEPPER (CAYENNE)

1   BAY LEAF

1   CAN (14½ OUNCES) DICED TOMATOES

1   CUP HALF-AND-HALF OR LIGHT CREAM

2   TABLESPOONS BRANDY OR DRY SHERRY

FRESH CHIVES FOR GARNISH

1   Shell and devein shrimp, reserving shells.

2   In 5-quart Dutch oven, melt 1 tablespoon butter or margarine over medium heat. Add shrimp shells and cook 5 minutes, stirring often.

3   Add chicken broth, wine, and water; heat to boiling over high heat. Reduce heat to low; cover and simmer 15 minutes. Strain broth mixture into 4-cup measuring cup or small bowl, pressing on shells with spoon to extract any remaining liquid. Discard shells.

4   In same Dutch oven, melt remaining 2 tablespoons butter or margarine over medium-high heat. Add shrimp and cook until they turn opaque throughout, about 3 minutes, stirring occasionally. With slotted spoon, transfer shrimp to another small bowl. Add carrots, celery, and onion; cook, stirring occasionally, 10 to 12 minutes, until lightly browned.

5   Return broth mixture to Dutch oven; add rice, salt, ground red pepper, and bay leaf. Heat to boiling over high heat. Reduce heat to low; cover and simmer 20 minutes or until rice is very tender. Add tomatoes with their juice and cook 10 minutes longer. Remove Dutch oven from heat; discard bay leaf and add shrimp.

6   In blender, at low speed, with center part of cover removed to allow steam to escape, blend shrimp mixture in small batches until pureed and very smooth. Pour pureed soup into large bowl after each batch.

7 Return soup to Dutch oven and add half-and-half and brandy; heat through over medium heat (do not boil or soup may curdle). Garnish each serving with fresh chives.

EACH SERVING: ABOUT 145 CALORIES | 10 G PROTEIN | 9 G CARBOHYDRATE | 7 G TOTAL FAT (2 G SATURATED) | 65 MG CHOLESTEROL | 750 MG SODIUM

TOMATO SOUP

A sensational way to use up every last ripe summer tomato when flavor will be at its peak. For a creamier version, stir in heavy or light cream or plain yogurt to taste.

ACTIVE TIME: 20 MINUTES · **TOTAL TIME:** 1 HOUR, 30 MINUTES
MAKES: ABOUT 8 CUPS OR 8 FIRST-COURSE SERVINGS

1 TABLESPOON BUTTER OR MARGARINE	1 CAN (13¾ TO 14½ OUNCES) CHICKEN BROTH
1 MEDIUM ONION, DICED	¾ TEASPOON SALT
1 MEDIUM STALK CELERY, DICED	¼ TEASPOON COARSELY GROUND BLACK PEPPER
1 MEDIUM CARROT, PEELED AND DICED	
1 GARLIC CLOVE, CRUSHED WITH GARLIC PRESS	1 BAY LEAF
2 TEASPOONS FRESH THYME LEAVES	½ CUP WATER
4 POUNDS RIPE TOMATOES, CUT UP	SNIPPED CHIVES FOR GARNISH

1 In 5-quart Dutch oven, melt butter over low heat. Add onion, celery, and carrot; cook 10 minutes, until tender. Stir in garlic and thyme; cook 1 minute.
2 Add tomatoes, broth, salt, pepper, bay leaf, and water; heat to boiling over high heat. Reduce heat to medium-low and cook, uncovered, 45 minutes or until tomatoes are broken up and mixture has thickened slightly. Discard bay leaf.
3 In blender, with center part of cover removed to allow steam to escape, blend tomato mixture in small batches until pureed. Pour pureed soup into large bowl after each batch. Repeat with remaining mixture.
4 Refrigerate soup to serve cold. Or reheat soup in same Dutch oven to serve hot. Sprinkle with chives to serve.

EACH SERVING: ABOUT 80 CALORIES │ 3 G PROTEIN │ 13 G CARBOHYDRATE │ 3 G TOTAL FAT (1 G SATURATED) │ 0 MG CHOLESTEROL │ 410 MG SODIUM

CREAM OF MUSHROOM SOUP

This mushroom-laden soup is very versatile. Use one variety or a mix of favorites. Some flavorful possibilities are cremini, shiitake, and portobello.

ACTIVE TIME: 20 MINUTES · **TOTAL TIME:** 55 MINUTES

MAKES: ABOUT 6 CUPS OR 6 FIRST-COURSE SERVINGS

3 TABLESPOONS BUTTER OR MARGARINE

1 POUND MUSHROOMS, TRIMMED AND THINLY SLICED

1 MEDIUM ONION, THINLY SLICED

2 TABLESPOONS ALL-PURPOSE FLOUR

2 CUPS WATER

1 CAN (14½ OUNCES) CHICKEN BROTH

½ TEASPOON FRESH THYME OR ¼ TEASPOON DRIED THYME

½ TEASPOON SALT

⅛ TEASPOON GROUND BLACK PEPPER

½ CUP HEAVY OR WHIPPING CREAM

1 In 5-quart Dutch oven, melt 2 tablespoons butter over medium-high heat. Add mushrooms and cook, stirring occasionally, until mushrooms are tender and begin to brown, about 15 minutes. Transfer to bowl.

2 In same Dutch oven, melt remaining 1 tablespoon butter over medium heat. Add onion and cook until tender and golden, about 10 minutes.

3 Stir in flour until blended; cook 1 minute. Gradually stir in water, broth, thyme, salt, pepper, and half of mushrooms; heat to boiling, stirring constantly.

4 In blender, with center part of cover removed to allow steam to escape, puree mushroom mixture in small batches until smooth. Pour puree into bowl after each batch.

5 Return puree to clean Dutch oven; stir in cream and remaining mushrooms with their juice. Heat through (do not boil).

EACH SERVING: ABOUT 167 CALORIES | 3 G PROTEIN | 9 G CARBOHYDRATE, | 14 G TOTAL FAT (8 G SATURATED) | 43 MG CHOLESTEROL | 548 MG SODIUM

COOL CUCUMBER SOUP

Perfect for a hot summer night, you can whip up this refreshing no-cook soup in no time flat in your blender.

ACTIVE TIME: 10 MINUTES · **TOTAL TIME:** 10 MINUTES

MAKES: ABOUT 3 CUPS OR 4 FIRST-COURSE SERVINGS

3   CUCUMBERS (ABOUT 8 OUNCES EACH), PEELED, SEEDED, AND COARSELY CHOPPED

1   CUP PLAIN LOW-FAT YOGURT

¾   TEASPOON SALT

¼   TEASPOON COARSELY GROUND BLACK PEPPER

3   LARGE ICE CUBES (ABOUT ½ CUP)

1   CUP LOOSELY PACKED FRESH MINT LEAVES, COARSELY CHOPPED

THIN CUCUMBER SLICES FOR GARNISH

1 In blender, combine cucumbers, yogurt, salt, and pepper and blend until smooth.

2 With motor running and center part of cover removed, add ice cubes, 1 at a time. Add mint leaves and blend 5 seconds longer. If not serving right away, cover and refrigerate up to 1 day. Garnish with cucumber slices.

EACH SERVING: ABOUT 60 CALORIES | 4 G PROTEIN | 9 G CARBOHYDRATE | 1 G TOTAL FAT (1 G SATURATED) | 4 MG CHOLESTEROL | 495 MG SODIUM

PEACHY MELON SOUP

Be sure to use the ripest, most fragrant melon you can find. The soup is scrumptious garnished with slivers of prosciutto.

ACTIVE TIME: 15 MINUTES · **TOTAL TIME:** 15 MINUTES
MAKES: 4 CUPS OR 5 FIRST-COURSE OR DESSERT SERVINGS

1 LARGE CANTALOUPE (2½ POUNDS), CHILLED

1 CUP PEACH OR APRICOT NECTAR, CHILLED

1 TABLESPOON FRESH LIME JUICE

LIME SLICES FOR GARNISH

1 Cut cantaloupe in half. Scoop out and discard seeds. Cut away rind, then cut cantaloupe into bite-size pieces.

2 In blender, puree cantaloupe, peach nectar, and lime juice until smooth. Increase speed to high; blend 1 minute. If not serving right away, pour soup into bowl and refrigerate. To serve, garnish with lime slices.

EACH SERVING: ABOUT 67 CALORIES | 1 G PROTEIN | 17 G CARBOHYDRATE | 0 G TOTAL FAT (0 G SATURATED) | 0 MG CHOLESTEROL | 14 MG SODIUM

CREAMY BUTTERMILK-BEET SOUP

Just four ingredients—perfect when the last thing you want to do is cook.

ACTIVE TIME: 10 MINUTES · **TOTAL TIME:** 10 MINUTES
MAKES: ABOUT 4 CUPS OR 4 FIRST-COURSE SERVINGS

3 CUPS BUTTERMILK

1 CAN (14 ½ TO 15 OUNCES) BEETS, DRAINED

½ TEASPOON SALT

1 TABLESPOON MINCED FRESH DILL

DILL SPRIGS FOR GARNISH

In blender, combine buttermilk, beets, and salt; blend until smooth. Pour mixture into large bowl; stir in minced dill. If not serving right away, cover and refrigerate up to 1 day. Garnish with dill sprigs.

EACH SERVING: ABOUT 95 CALORIES | 7 G PROTEIN | 14 G CARBOHYDRATE | 2 G TOTAL FAT (1 G SATURATED) | 7 MG CHOLESTEROL | 655 MG SODIUM

TART CHERRY SOUP

When the weather turns hot, offer this refreshing chilled soup for dessert, as a first course, or for a light lunch. Tart cherries, also called pie cherries, are available frozen and canned. In season, use two pounds of pitted fresh tart cherries instead.

ACTIVE TIME: 5 MINUTES · **TOTAL TIME:** 20 MINUTES PLUS STANDING AND CHILLING
MAKES: 4 CUPS OR 4 FIRST-COURSE OR DESSERT SERVINGS

2½ CUPS RIESLING OR OTHER SEMIDRY WHITE WINE

2 CANS (16 OUNCES EACH) OR 1 JAR (32 OUNCES) PITTED TART (SOUR) CHERRIES, DRAINED, ⅓ CUP LIQUID RESERVED

⅓ CUP SUGAR

1½ TEASPOONS QUICK-COOKING TAPIOCA

6 STRIPS (3" BY ½" EACH) ORANGE PEEL

1 CINNAMON STICK (3 INCHES)

1 VANILLA BEAN, SPLIT, OR ½ TEASPOON VANILLA EXTRACT

6 WHOLE ALLSPICE BERRIES

6 WHOLE BLACK PEPPERCORNS

½ CUP SOUR CREAM

1 In nonreactive 2-quart saucepan, combine wine, ⅓ cup reserved cherry liquid (discard remaining liquid), sugar, tapioca, orange peel, cinnamon, vanilla bean (if using), allspice, and peppercorns. Heat to boiling over medium heat. Reduce heat; cover and simmer 7 minutes. Remove from heat and let stand 20 minutes. Strain through fine-mesh sieve set over bowl, pressing with back of spoon to push tapioca through; discard spices and peel. (You can rinse vanilla bean, let it dry, and use it to flavor sugar in a canister.) Add vanilla extract, if using.

2 Stir in cherries. Transfer soup in batches to blender and puree until smooth. Pour soup into bowl after each batch. With wire whisk, mix sour cream into soup until smooth. Cover and refrigerate about 4 hours or until cold.

EACH SERVING: ABOUT 317 CALORIES | 3 G PROTEIN | 41 G CARBOHYDRATE | 6 G TOTAL FAT (4 G SATURATED) | 13 MG CHOLESTEROL | 45 MG SODIUM

PEAR AND RED WINE SOUP

Serve this chilled soup before a hearty main course. As with all fruit soups, make it with fully ripened fruit at its peak of flavor.

ACTIVE TIME: 10 MINUTES · **TOTAL TIME:** 30 TO 35 MINUTES PLUS CHILLING
MAKES: ABOUT 3½ CUPS OR 4 FIRST-COURSE SERVINGS

1 CUP DRY RED WINE	1 LEMON
1 CUP WATER	1½ POUNDS RIPE PEARS, PEELED, CORED,
½ CUP SUGAR	AND CUT INTO QUARTERS

1 In nonreactive 2-quart saucepan, combine wine, water, and sugar; heat to boiling over high heat, stirring frequently, until sugar has dissolved.

2 Meanwhile, with vegetable peeler, from lemon, remove two 3-inch strips peel; squeeze 1 tablespoon juice.

3 Add pears and lemon peel to saucepan; heat to boiling over high heat. Reduce heat and simmer until pears are very tender, 10 to 15 minutes.

4 In blender, with center part of cover removed to allow steam to escape, puree one-fourth of pear mixture until smooth. Pour pureed soup into bowl. Repeat with remaining mixture. Stir in lemon juice. Cover soup and refrigerate at least 4 hours or until very cold.

EACH SERVING: ABOUT 234 CALORIES | 1 G PROTEIN | 50 G CARBOHYDRATE | 1 G TOTAL FAT (0 G SATURATED) | 0 MG CHOLESTEROL | 3 MG SODIUM

CREAMY ITALIAN WHITE-BEAN SOUP

A perfect marriage of canned beans and fresh spinach, with a squeeze of fresh lemon juice to brighten the flavors.

ACTIVE TIME: 15 MINUTES · **TOTAL TIME:** 55 MINUTES

MAKES: ABOUT 6 CUPS OR 4 MAIN-DISH SERVINGS

1 TABLESPOON VEGETABLE OIL

1 MEDIUM ONION, FINELY CHOPPED

1 MEDIUM STALK CELERY, FINELY CHOPPED

1 GARLIC CLOVE, MINCED

2 CANS (15½ TO 19 OUNCES EACH) WHITE KIDNEY BEANS (CANNELLINI), RINSED AND DRAINED

1 CAN (14½ OUNCES) CHICKEN BROTH

¼ TEASPOON COARSELY GROUND BLACK PEPPER

⅛ TEASPOON DRIED THYME

2 CUPS WATER

1 BUNCH (10 TO 12 OUNCES) SPINACH

1 TABLESPOON FRESH LEMON JUICE

FRESHLY GRATED PARMESAN CHEESE (OPTIONAL)

1 In 3-quart saucepan, heat vegetable oil over medium heat until hot. Add onion and celery and cook 5 to 8 minutes, until tender, stirring occasionally. Add garlic; cook 30 seconds, stirring. Add beans, chicken broth, pepper, thyme, and water; heat to boiling over high heat. Reduce heat to low; simmer, uncovered, 15 minutes.

2 Meanwhile, discard tough stems from spinach; thinly slice leaves.

3 With slotted spoon, remove 2 cups bean-and-vegetable mixture from soup; set aside. In blender at low speed, with center part of cover removed to allow steam to escape, blend remaining soup in small batches until smooth. Pour pureed soup into large bowl after each batch.

4 Return soup to saucepan; stir in reserved beans and vegetables. Heat to boiling over high heat, stirring occasionally. Stir in spinach and cook 1 minute or until wilted. Stir in lemon juice and remove from heat. Serve with Parmesan cheese, if you like.

EACH SERVING WITHOUT PARMESAN: ABOUT 295 CALORIES | 18 G PROTEIN | 46 G CARBO-HYDRATE | 5 G TOTAL FAT (1 G SATURATED) | 0 MG CHOLESTEROL | 945 MG SODIUM

VICHYSSOISE

This luxurious soup, traditionally served cold, is just as delicious hot (just call it cream of potato and leek soup). Either way, serve in small cups and garnish with freshly chopped chives.

ACTIVE TIME: 20 MINUTES · **TOTAL TIME:** 1 HOUR, 15 MINUTES PLUS CHILLING

MAKES: ABOUT 8 CUPS OR 8 FIRST-COURSE SERVINGS

4	MEDIUM LEEKS (1¼ POUNDS)	½	CUP WATER
2	TABLESPOONS BUTTER OR MARGARINE	1	TEASPOON SALT
		¼	TEASPOON GROUND BLACK PEPPER
1	POUND ALL-PURPOSE POTATOES (3 MEDIUM), PEELED AND THINLY SLICED	1	CUP MILK
		½	CUP HEAVY OR WHIPPING CREAM
2	CANS (14½ OUNCES EACH) CHICKEN BROTH		

1 Cut off roots and trim dark green tops from leeks; cut each leek lengthwise in half. Cut enough of white and pale green parts crosswise into ¼-inch pieces to equal 4½ cups. (Reserve any leftover leeks for another use.) Rinse leeks in large bowl of cold water, swishing to remove sand; transfer to colander to drain, leaving sand in bottom of bowl.

2 In 4-quart saucepan, melt butter over medium heat; add leeks and cook, stirring occasionally, 8 to 10 minutes. Add potatoes, broth, water, salt, and pepper; heat to boiling over high heat. Reduce heat; cover and simmer for 30 minutes.

3 In blender, with center part of cover removed to allow steam to escape, puree half of mixture until smooth. Pour pureed soup into large bowl. Repeat with remaining mixture.

4 Stir milk and cream into puree. To serve hot, return soup to same clean saucepan and heat through over low heat (do not boil). To serve cold, cover and refrigerate at least 4 hours or until very cold.

EACH SERVING: ABOUT 161 CALORIES | 4 G PROTEIN | 14 G CARBOHYDRATE | 10 G TOTAL FAT (6 G SATURATED) | 32 MG CHOLESTEROL | 778 MG SODIUM

SPICED LENTIL SOUP

Based on an Indian classic, this thick and hearty soup is bound to become a staple in your repertoire. Lentils, unlike other dried legumes, don't require presoaking, so this can be prepared in less time than most bean soups.

ACTIVE TIME: 30 MINUTES · **TOTAL TIME:** 1 HOUR, 40 MINUTES

MAKES: 11 CUPS OR 5 MAIN-DISH SERVINGS

---

2   TABLESPOONS OLIVE OIL

4   CARROTS, PEELED AND FINELY CHOPPED

2   LARGE STALKS CELERY, FINELY CHOPPED

1   LARGE ONION (12 OUNCES), FINELY CHOPPED

1   MEDIUM GRANNY SMITH APPLE, PEELED, CORED, AND FINELY CHOPPED

1   TABLESPOON GRATED, PEELED FRESH GINGER

1   GARLIC CLOVE, CRUSHED WITH GARLIC PRESS

2   TEASPOONS CURRY POWDER

¾   TEASPOON GROUND CUMIN

¾   TEASPOON GROUND CORIANDER

1   PACKAGE (16 OUNCES) LENTILS, RINSED AND PICKED THROUGH

5   CUPS WATER

2   CANS (14½ OUNCES EACH) VEGETABLE OR CHICKEN BROTH

¼   CUP CHOPPED FRESH CILANTRO

½   TEASPOON SALT

PLAIN LOW-FAT YOGURT

1 In 5-quart Dutch oven, heat oil over medium-high heat. Add carrots, celery, onion, and apple; cook, stirring occasionally, until lightly browned, 10 to 15 minutes.

2 Add ginger, garlic, curry powder, cumin, and coriander; cook, stirring, 1 minute.

3 Add lentils, water, and broth; heat to boiling over high heat. Reduce heat; cover and simmer, stirring occasionally, until lentils are tender, 45 to 55 minutes.

4 In blender, with center part of cover removed to allow steam to escape, blend 5 cups soup in batches. Pour pureed soup into large bowl. Return soup to Dutch oven. Heat through. Stir in cilantro and salt. Ladle soup into 5 soup bowls; top each with dollops of yogurt.

EACH SERVING: ABOUT 441 CALORIES | 29 G PROTEIN | 71 G CARBOHYDRATE | 8 G TOTAL FAT (1 G SATURATED) | 0 MG CHOLESTEROL | 963 MG SODIUM

SPLIT-PEA SOUP WITH HAM

On a wintry day, nothing satisfies more than an old-fashioned favorite like split-pea soup.

ACTIVE TIME: 10 MINUTES · **TOTAL TIME:** 1 HOUR, 25 MINUTES TO 1 HOUR, 35 MINUTES
MAKES: 12 CUPS OR 6 MAIN-DISH SERVINGS

4	STRIPS BACON	1	PACKAGE (16 OUNCES) DRY SPLIT PEAS, RINSED AND PICKED THROUGH
2	WHITE TURNIPS (6 OUNCES EACH), PEELED AND CHOPPED (OPTIONAL)	5	CUPS WATER
2	CARROTS, PEELED AND FINELY CHOPPED	2	CANS (14½ OUNCES EACH) CHICKEN BROTH
2	STALKS CELERY, FINELY CHOPPED	1	BAY LEAF
1	MEDIUM ONION, FINELY CHOPPED	¾	TEASPOON SALT
		¼	TEASPOON GROUND ALLSPICE

1 In 5-quart Dutch oven, cook bacon over medium-high heat until crisp. Remove bacon with slotted spoon to paper towels; drain and set aside.
2 Discard all but 2 tablespoons drippings from Dutch oven. Add turnips, if using, carrots, celery, and onion; cook, stirring frequently, until carrots are tender-crisp, about 10 minutes. Add split peas, water, chicken broth, bay leaf, salt, and allspice; heat to boiling over high heat. Reduce heat; cover and simmer 45 to 55 minutes.
3 Discard bay leaf. In blender, with center part of cover removed to allow steam to escape, blend soup in 2 batches; return each batch to Dutch oven. Heat through. Ladle soup into 6 bowls. Crumble reserved bacon; sprinkle over each serving.

EACH SERVING: ABOUT 358 CALORIES | 22 G PROTEIN | 51 G CARBOHYDRATE | 8 G TOTAL FAT (3 G SATURATED) | 8 MG CHOLESTEROL | 960 MG SODIUM

POTATO SOUP WITH BACON AND PARMESAN

This stick-to-your-ribs soup is the perfect foil against any winter chill. Pureeing some of the cooked potatoes gives it a wonderful thick texture.

ACTIVE TIME: 25 MINUTES · **TOTAL TIME:** 1 HOUR

MAKES: ABOUT 8 CUPS OR 8 FIRST-COURSE SERVINGS

3 SLICES BACON, FINELY CHOPPED

2 MEDIUM ONIONS, CHOPPED

1 LARGE GARLIC CLOVE, MINCED

¾ TEASPOON SALT

¼ TEASPOON DRIED ROSEMARY, CRUMBLED

¼ TEASPOON FRESHLY GROUND PEPPER

2 POUNDS BAKING POTATOES (3 LARGE), PEELED AND CUT INTO ½-INCH CUBES

2 CANS (14 ½ OUNCES EACH) CHICKEN BROTH

1 CUP WATER

1 SMALL BUNCH SPINACH (8 OUNCES) STEMS REMOVED, LEAVES COARSELY CHOPPED (ABOUT 4 CUPS)

¾ CUP GRATED PARMESAN CHEESE

½ CUP MILK

1 In 5-quart Dutch oven, cook bacon over medium heat until browned. With slotted spoon, transfer bacon to a small bowl.

2 To bacon drippings in Dutch oven, add onions and cook, stirring, until onions are golden, about 8 minutes. Stir in garlic, salt, rosemary, and pepper; cook, stirring, 1 minute.

3 Stir in potatoes, broth, and water; heat to boiling over high heat. Reduce heat; cover and simmer until potatoes are just tender, 10 to 15 minutes.

4 Remove and set aside 2 cups soup. Stir spinach into soup remaining in Dutch oven. Bring to a simmer; cover and simmer until spinach is wilted, about 3 minutes.

5 Meanwhile, transfer reserved soup to blender. With center part of cover removed to allow steam to escape, blend until smooth.

6 Stir bacon, pureed soup, Parmesan cheese, and milk into Dutch oven. Heat through (do not boil). Ladle into 8 soup bowls.

EACH SERVING: ABOUT 240 CALORIES | 8 G PROTEIN | 26 G CARBOHYDRATE | 12 G TOTAL FAT (5 G SATURATED) | 18 MG CHOLESTEROL | 928 MG SODIUM

CARIBBEAN BLACK-BEAN SOUP

Our new take on black-bean soup is made with fresh cilantro for great flavor and spiced with jalapeños for heat.

ACTIVE TIME: 45 MINUTES · **TOTAL TIME:** 3 HOURS, 15 MINUTES PLUS SOAKING BEANS
MAKES: ABOUT 10 CUPS OR 10 FIRST-COURSE SERVINGS

1 POUND DRY BLACK BEANS

3 TABLESPOONS VEGETABLE OIL

2 MEDIUM RED ONIONS, CHOPPED

4 JALAPEÑO CHILES, SEEDED AND MINCED

2 TABLESPOONS MINCED, PEELED FRESH GINGER

4 GARLIC CLOVES, MINCED

½ TEASPOON GROUND ALLSPICE

½ TEASPOON DRIED THYME

12 CUPS WATER

1½ POUNDS SWEET POTATOES (2 MEDIUM), PEELED AND CUT INTO ¾-INCH CHUNKS

1 TABLESPOON BROWN SUGAR

2 TEASPOONS SALT

6 GREEN ONIONS, FINELY CHOPPED

½ CUP CHOPPED FRESH CILANTRO LEAVES

LIME WEDGES

1 Rinse beans with cold running water and discard any stones or shriveled beans. In large bowl, place beans and enough water to cover by 2 inches. Cover and let stand at room temperature overnight. (Or, in 6-quart saucepot, place beans and **enough water to cover by 2 inches**. Heat to boiling over high heat; cook 2 minutes. Remove from heat; cover and let stand 1 hour.) Drain and rinse beans.

2 In 5-quart Dutch oven, heat vegetable oil over medium heat. Add onions and cook, stirring occasionally, 5 minutes or until tender. Add jalapeños, ginger, garlic, allspice, and thyme, and cook, stirring, 3 minutes.

3 Add drained beans and the 12 cups water to Dutch oven; heat to boiling over high heat. Reduce heat and simmer 1½ hours. Add sweet potatoes, brown sugar, and salt and cook 30 minutes. Add green onions and cook mixture 3 minutes longer.

4 Transfer 2 cups bean mixture to blender; cover, with center part of cover removed to let steam escape, and puree until smooth. Return puree to Dutch oven and stir in cilantro. Serve with lime wedges.

EACH SERVING: ABOUT 270 CALORIES | 12 G PROTEIN | 47 G CARBOHYDRATE | 5 G TOTAL FAT (1 G SATURATED) | 0 MG CHOLESTEROL | 481 MG SODIUM

COLD AVOCADO SOUP

A refreshing and elegant lunch or first course. Place a few corn tortilla chips in each bowl for an additional crunchy garnish.

ACTIVE TIME: 25 MINUTES · **TOTAL TIME:** 25 MINUTES

MAKES: ABOUT 5 CUPS OR 6 FIRST-COURSE SERVINGS

½ SMALL GARLIC CLOVE

1 SMALL JALAPEÑO, SEEDED AND COARSELY CHOPPED

3 RIPE AVOCADOS, HALVED, PITTED (ABOUT 9 OUNCES EACH)

1 CAN (14½ OUNCES) CHICKEN BROTH

1¼ TO 1½ CUPS COLD WATER

1 CUP PLAIN LOW-FAT YOGURT

¼ CUP FRESH LIME OR LEMON JUICE

1 TEASPOON SALT

½ CUP LOOSELY PACKED BASIL LEAVES

½ CUP LOOSELY PACKED CILANTRO LEAVES

½ CUP LOOSELY PACKED MINT LEAVES

1 PLUM TOMATO, SEEDED AND FINELY CHOPPED, FOR GARNISH

1 In blender, with motor running, drop garlic and jalapeño through small hole in top and blend until minced.

2 With a tablespoon, scoop avocados into blender. Add chicken broth, 1 cup plus 2 tablespoons water, ½ cup plain yogurt, lime juice, and ¾ teaspoon salt, blend until smooth. Pour into a bowl, cover tightly with plastic wrap against surface, and refrigerate until cold, at least 4 hours.

3 In blender, combine remaining 2 tablespoons water, ½ cup yogurt, ¼ teaspoon salt, basil, cilantro, and mint and blend until smooth. Pour puree into a small bowl, cover, and refrigerate.

4 Before serving, stir up to ¼ cup water into soup if too thick. Garnish soup with dollops of herb puree and sprinkle with tomato.

EACH SERVING: ABOUT 194 CALORIES | 5 G PROTEIN | 11 G CARBOHYDRATE | 16 G TOTAL FAT (3 G SATURATED) | 2 MG CHOLESTEROL | 707 MG SODIUM

DIPS, SAUCES & SALAD DRESSINGS

Green Goddess (page 136), Russian (page 134), and Poppy Seed Dressing (page 135)

ROASTED RED PEPPER AND WALNUT DIP

This delicious Middle Eastern dip is a perfect blend of sweetness and tang.

ACTIVE TIME: 30 MINUTES · **TOTAL TIME:** 40 MINUTES PLUS COOLING
MAKES: 1½ CUPS

4   MEDIUM RED PEPPERS

½   CUP WALNUTS

½   TEASPOON GROUND CUMIN

2   SLICES FIRM WHITE BREAD, TORN
    INTO PIECES

2   TABLESPOONS RASPBERRY OR
    BALSAMIC VINEGAR

1   TABLESPOON OLIVE OIL

½   TEASPOON SALT

⅛   TEASPOON GROUND RED PEPPER
    (CAYENNE)

TOASTED PITA TRIANGLES

1   Line broiling pan with foil. Broil peppers at closest position to source of heat, turning occasionally, 10 minutes or until charred and blistered all over. Remove from broiler. Wrap foil around peppers and allow to steam at room temperature 15 minutes or until cool enough to handle.

2   Meanwhile, turn oven control to 350°F. Spread walnuts in metal baking pan and bake 8 to 10 minutes, until toasted. In dry 1-quart saucepan, toast cumin over low heat 1 to 2 minutes, until very fragrant.

3   Remove peppers from foil. Peel off skin; discard skin and seeds. Cut peppers into large pieces. In blender, blend walnuts until ground. Add roasted peppers, cumin, bread, vinegar, olive oil, salt, and ground red pepper; blend until smooth, frequently stirring or scraping with spatula. Transfer to bowl. Cover and refrigerate if not serving right away. Remove from refrigerator 30 minutes before serving. Serve with toasted pita triangles.

EACH TABLESPOON DIP: ABOUT 25 CALORIES | 0 G PROTEIN | 2 G CARBOHYDRATE | 2 G TO-TAL FAT (0 G SATURATED) | 0 MG CHOLESTEROL | 40 MG SODIUM

BLACK BEAN DIP

Mix and match white- and blue-corn tortilla chips to serve with this spicy Tex-Mex bean dip. You can substitute canned pinto beans for black beans, if that's what you have in your pantry.

ACTIVE TIME: 5 MINUTES · **TOTAL TIME:** 10 MINUTES
MAKES: ABOUT 2 CUPS

4   GARLIC CLOVES, PEELED

1   CAN (15 TO 19 OUNCES) BLACK BEANS, RINSED AND DRAINED

2   TABLESPOONS TOMATO PASTE

2   TABLESPOONS OLIVE OIL

5   TEASPOONS FRESH LIME JUICE

½   TEASPOON GROUND CUMIN

½   TEASPOON GROUND CORIANDER

¼   TEASPOON SALT

⅛   TEASPOON GROUND RED PEPPER (CAYENNE)

1   In 1-quart saucepan, place garlic and enough water to cover; heat to boiling over high heat. Reduce heat to low; cover and simmer 3 minutes to blanch garlic. Reserve **¾ cup blanching water**. Drain garlic.

2   In blender, combine ½ cup reserved water and garlic; blend until smooth. Add beans, tomato paste, oil, lime juice, cumin, coriander, salt, and ground red pepper. Blend until smooth, adding remaining reserved water if necessary, until mixture reaches dipping consistency. Spoon dip into bowl; cover and refrigerate up to 2 days.

EACH TABLESPOON DIP: ABOUT 18 CALORIES │ 1 G PROTEIN │ 3 G CARBOHYDRATE
1 G TOTAL FAT (0 G SATURATED) │ 0 MG CHOLESTEROL │ 54 MG SODIUM

CREAMY BAGNA CAUDA

Serve this warm anchovy-flavored Italian dip with a variety of raw vegetables, such as red and yellow bell pepper, carrots, celery, zucchini, broccoli, and radishes. Be sure to cut the vegetables into pieces thick enough to hold the sauce.

ACTIVE TIME: 10 MINUTES · **TOTAL TIME:** 35 MINUTES
MAKES: ⅔ CUP

⅔ CUP HEAVY OR WHIPPING CREAM

¼ CUP PEELED GARLIC CLOVES (FROM ABOUT 1 SMALL HEAD)

1 TEASPOON ANCHOVY PASTE

⅛ TEASPOON GROUND RED PEPPER (CAYENNE)

1 In 1-quart saucepan, heat cream and garlic over medium-low heat to boiling. Reduce heat and simmer, covered, until garlic is very soft, about 25 minutes.

2 Transfer mixture to blender; add anchovy paste and ground red pepper. Blend until smooth and thick. Serve warm.

EACH TABLESPOON DIP: ABOUT 50 CALORIES | 1 G PROTEIN | 1 G CARBOHYDRATE
5 G TOTAL FAT (3 G SATURATED) | 19 MG CHOLESTEROL | 18 MG SODIUM

MANGO CURRY DIP

This is a new take on the tried-and-true appetizer of mango chutney atop cream cheese. Our sour-cream based version is delicious as a dip for vegetables and as a sandwich spread for ham or turkey.

ACTIVE TIME: 5 MINUTES · **TOTAL TIME:** 5 MINUTES

MAKES: ABOUT 1½ CUPS

- 2 PACKAGES (3 OUNCES EACH) CREAM CHEESE, SOFTENED
- ½ CUP SOUR CREAM
- ¼ CUP MANGO CHUTNEY, CHOPPED
- 2 TEASPOONS CURRY POWDER
- 1 TEASPOON GROUND CORIANDER
- ½ TEASPOON GROUND CUMIN
- ½ TEASPOON GROUND GINGER
- ½ TEASPOON SALT

In blender, combine cream cheese, sour cream, chutney, curry powder, coriander, cumin, ginger, and salt and blend until smooth. Spoon dip into bowl; cover and refrigerate up to 2 days.

EACH TABLESPOON DIP: ABOUT 41 CALORIES | 1 G PROTEIN | 2 G CARBOHYDRATE 3 G TOTAL FAT (2 G SATURATED) | 10 MG CHOLESTEROL | 72 MG SODIUM

ROASTED EGGPLANT DIP WITH HERBS

A great party starter, this dip has the smoky flavor of roasted eggplant balanced by the sparkle of lemon juice and the freshness of mint and parsley.

ACTIVE TIME: 15 MINUTES · **TOTAL TIME:** 1 HOUR, 25 MINUTES PLUS COOLING
MAKES: ABOUT 2 CUPS

2 SMALL EGGPLANTS (1 POUND EACH)
2 GARLIC CLOVES, THINLY SLICED
2 TABLESPOONS OLIVE OIL
4 TEASPOONS FRESH LEMON JUICE
1 TEASPOON SALT

¼ TEASPOON GROUND BLACK PEPPER
2 TABLESPOONS CHOPPED FRESH PARSLEY
2 TABLESPOONS CHOPPED FRESH MINT
TOASTED PITA TRIANGLES

1 Preheat oven to 400°F. With knife, cut slits all over eggplants; insert garlic slices in slits. Place eggplants on jelly-roll pan and roast until collapsed and tender, about 1 hour.

2 When cool enough to handle, cut eggplants in half. Scoop out flesh and place in colander set over bowl; discard skin. Let drain 10 minutes.

3 Transfer eggplant to blender. Add oil, lemon juice, salt, and pepper; pulse to coarsely chop. Add parsley and mint, pulsing to combine. Spoon into bowl; cover and refrigerate up to 4 hours. Serve with toasted pita triangles.

EACH TABLESPOON DIP: ABOUT 11 CALORIES | 0 G PROTEIN | 1 G CARBOHYDRATE
1 G TOTAL FAT (0 G SATURATED) | 0 MG CHOLESTEROL | 73 MG SODIUM

CHICKEN LIVER PÂTÉ

This exquisite silky-smooth pâté is seasoned the traditional way—with thyme and brandy. For the best flavor, refrigerate the pâté at least three hours before serving.

ACTIVE TIME: 25 MINUTES · **TOTAL TIME:** 45 MINUTES PLUS CHILLING
MAKES: ABOUT 1½ CUPS

2   TABLESPOONS BUTTER
     OR MARGARINE

1   SMALL ONION, FINELY CHOPPED

1   GARLIC CLOVE, FINELY CHOPPED

1   POUND CHICKEN LIVERS, TRIMMED

2   TABLESPOONS BRANDY

½   CUP HEAVY OR WHIPPING CREAM

½   TEASPOON SALT

¼   TEASPOON DRIED THYME

¼   TEASPOON GROUND BLACK PEPPER

ASSORTED CRACKERS, TOAST, OR THINLY SLICED APPLES

1   In 10-inch skillet, melt butter over medium-high heat. Add onion and cook, stirring frequently, until tender and golden, about 10 minutes. Stir in garlic and livers and cook until livers are lightly browned but still pink inside, about 5 minutes. Stir in brandy; cook 5 minutes.

2   In blender, puree chicken-liver mixture, cream, salt, thyme, and pepper until smooth, stopping blender occasionally and scraping down side with rubber spatula.

3   Spoon mixture into small bowl; cover and refrigerate at least 3 hours or up to overnight. Let stand 30 minutes at room temperature before serving. Serve with crackers, toast, or apples.

EACH TABLESPOON DIP: ABOUT 54 CALORIES | 4 G PROTEIN | 1 G CARBOHYDRATE
4 G TOTAL FAT (2 G SATURATED) | 92 MG CHOLESTEROL | 75 MG SODIUM

HUMMUS

This Middle Eastern classic is usually made from garbanzo beans, also known as chick peas. Serve it with pita triangles and whole radishes, cucumber slices, and carrot sticks.

ACTIVE TIME: 20 MINUTES · **TOTAL TIME:** 20 MINUTES
MAKES: ABOUT 2 CUPS

1 CAN (15 TO 19 OUNCES) GARBANZO BEANS, RINSED AND DRAINED

½ CUP TAHINI (SESAME SEED PASTE)

⅓ CUP WATER

¼ CUP FRESH LEMON JUICE

½ TEASPOON GROUND CUMIN

½ TEASPOON SALT

¼ TEASPOON COARSELY GROUND BLACK PEPPER

1 GARLIC CLOVE, CHOPPED

1 TABLESPOON EXTRAVIRGIN OLIVE OIL

1 TABLESPOON CHOPPED PARSLEY LEAVES

PINCH PAPRIKA

1 In blender, combine garbanzo beans, tahini, water, lemon juice, cumin, salt, pepper, and garlic, and blend until smooth. Cover and refrigerate if not serving right away.

2 To serve, spoon Hummus onto platter. Drizzle with olive oil and sprinkle with parsley and paprika.

EACH TABLESPOON DIP: ABOUT 46 CALORIES | 2 G PROTEIN | 3 G CARBOHYDRATE
3 G TOTAL FAT (0 G SATURATED) | 0 MG CHOLESTEROL | 68 MG SODIUM

CAESAR SALAD DRESSING

Just toss the dressing with crisp romaine lettuce leaves and toasted croutons and you have a classic Caesar salad. Make it a main dish by adding grilled chicken or shrimp.

ACTIVE TIME: 10 MINUTES · **TOTAL TIME:** 10 MINUTES
MAKES: ¾ CUP

- 2 OUNCES PARMESAN CHEESE, CUT INTO SMALL CHUNKS
- 1 LARGE GARLIC CLOVE, PEELED
- ¼ CUP MAYONNAISE
- 3 TABLESPOONS FRESH LEMON JUICE
- 3 TABLESPOONS OLIVE OIL
- 2 TABLESPOONS WATER
- 1 TABLESPOON DIJON MUSTARD
- 2 TEASPOONS ANCHOVY PASTE
- 1 TEASPOON WORCESTERSHIRE SAUCE
- ⅛ TEASPOON FRESHLY GROUND BLACK PEPPER

1 In blender, combine Parmesan cheese and garlic. Blend until cheese is finely grated.

2 Add mayonnaise, lemon juice, olive oil, water, mustard, anchovy paste, Worcestershire, and pepper and blend until mixture is combined. Transfer to bowl or jar. Refrigerate at least 1 hour to allow flavors to blend.

EACH TABLESPOON: ABOUT 89 CALORIES | 2 G PROTEIN | 1 G CARBOHYDRATE | 9 G TOTAL FAT (2 G SATURATED) | 7 MG CHOLESTEROL | 150 MG SODIUM

TAHINI DRESSING

Try this sesame-paste dressing on sautéed or broiled chicken or vegetables, as well as on salads.

ACTIVE TIME: 10 MINUTES · **TOTAL TIME:** 10 MINUTES

MAKES: ABOUT ¾ CUP

⅓ CUP TAHINI (SESAME SEED PASTE)

2 TABLESPOONS FRESH LEMON JUICE

4 TEASPOONS SOY SAUCE

1 TABLESPOON HONEY (OPTIONAL)

½ SMALL GARLIC CLOVE, MINCED

½ TEASPOON GROUND BLACK PEPPER

In blender, combine tahini, lemon juice, soy sauce, honey if using, garlic, and pepper. Blend until smooth. Cover and refrigerate up to 2 days.

EACH TABLESPOON: ABOUT 41 CALORIES | 1 G PROTEIN | 2 G CARBOHYDRATE | 4 G TOTAL FAT (0 G SATURATED) | 0 MG CHOLESTEROL | 122 MG SODIUM

JAPANESE MISO VINAIGRETTE

Miso comes in white, red or brown. The flavor intensifies as the color darkens—any one will make a tasty dressing.

ACTIVE TIME: 10 MINUTES · **TOTAL TIME:** 10 MINUTES

MAKES: ABOUT 1 CUP

2 TABLESPOONS MISO (FERMENTED SOYBEAN PASTE)

½ CUP RICE VINEGAR

¼ CUP OLIVE OIL

1 TABLESPOON MINCED, PEELED FRESH GINGER

1 TABLESPOON SUGAR

In small bowl, with wire whisk, stir miso into vinegar until smooth. In blender, combine miso mixture, oil, ginger, and sugar; puree until smooth. Transfer to bowl or jar. Cover and refrigerate up to 3 days.

EACH TABLESPOON: ABOUT 38 CALORIES | 0 G PROTEIN | 1 G CARBOHYDRATE | 4 G TOTAL FAT (0 G SATURATED) | 0 MG CHOLESTEROL | 78 MG SODIUM

CLASSIC FRENCH VINAIGRETTE

Why use bottled dressings, when it is so quick and easy to whip up a fresh homemade vinaigrette in just minutes?

ACTIVE TIME: 5 MINUTES · **TOTAL TIME:** 5 MINUTES

MAKES: ABOUT ¾ CUP

¼ CUP RED WINE VINEGAR

1 TABLESPOON DIJON MUSTARD

¾ TEASPOON SALT

½ TEASPOON COARSELY GROUND BLACK PEPPER

½ CUP OLIVE OIL

In blender, combine vinegar, mustard, salt, and pepper and blend until combined. Remove center of cover (or cover) and, at low speed, very slowly pour in oil in steady stream, blending until mixed. Transfer to jar; cover and refrigerate up to 1 week.

EACH TABLESPOON: ABOUT 83 CALORIES | 0 G PROTEIN | 0 G CARBOHYDRATE | 9 G TOTAL FAT (1 G SATURATED) | 0 MG CHOLESTEROL | 153 MG SODIUM

MUSTARD-SHALLOT VINAIGRETTE

MAKES: ABOUT ¾ CUP

Prepare as directed but add **1 tablespoon minced shallot**. Cover and refrigerate up to 1 day.

BLUE CHEESE VINAIGRETTE

MAKES: ABOUT 1 CUP

Prepare as directed but add **2 ounces blue cheese, crumbled (½ cup)**. Cover and refrigerate dressing up to 2 days.

TOMATO VINAIGRETTE

Perfect spooned over sliced tomatoes, spinach salad, or mixed greens.

ACTIVE TIME: 15 MINUTES · **TOTAL TIME:** 15 MINUTES
MAKES: 1 CUP

1	SMALL TOMATO (4 OUNCES), PEELED AND COARSELY CHOPPED	2	TEASPOONS DIJON MUSTARD WITH SEEDS
1	SMALL SHALLOT, CUT IN HALF	1	TEASPOON CHOPPED FRESH OREGANO
2	TABLESPOONS OLIVE OIL	1	TEASPOON SUGAR
1	TABLESPOON RED WINE VINEGAR	¼	TEASPOON SALT
1	TABLESPOON BALSAMIC VINEGAR	¼	TEASPOON GROUND BLACK PEPPER

In blender, combine tomato, shallot, oil, both vinegars, mustard, oregano, sugar, salt, and pepper; puree just until smooth. Transfer to jar; cover and refrigerate up to 1 day.

EACH TABLESPOON: ABOUT 19 CALORIES | 0 G PROTEIN 1 G CARBOHYDRATE | 2 G TOTAL FAT (0 G SATURATED) | 0 MG CHOLESTEROL | 51 MG SODIUM

RUSSIAN DRESSING

Actually American in origin, early versions included Russian caviar.

ACTIVE TIME: 10 MINUTES · **TOTAL TIME:** 10 MINUTES
MAKES: ABOUT 1 CUP

¾	CUP MAYONNAISE	¼	TEASPOON DRY MUSTARD
¼	CUP KETCHUP	¼	TEASPOON WORCESTERSHIRE SAUCE
2	TABLESPOONS FRESH PARSLEY LEAVES	3	DROPS HOT PEPPER SAUCE
1	TABLESPOON GRATED ONION (OPTIONAL)		

In blender, combine mayonnaise, ketchup, parsley, onion if using, mustard, Worcestershire, and hot pepper sauce; blend until well mixed. Transfer to jar; cover and refrigerate up to 3 days.

EACH TABLESPOON: ABOUT 78 CALORIES | 0 G PROTEIN | 1 G CARBOHYDRATE | 8 G TOTAL FAT (1 G SATURATED) | 6 MG CHOLESTEROL | 105 MG SODIUM

POPPY SEED DRESSING

In the mood for a sweet-and-sour dressing? Spoon this gem over iceberg lettuce wedges or a colorful fresh fruit salad.

ACTIVE TIME: 10 MINUTES · **TOTAL TIME:** 10 MINUTES
MAKES: 1½ CUPS

1 CUP VEGETABLE OIL	1 TABLESPOON POPPY SEEDS
⅓ CUP CIDER VINEGAR	1 TEASPOON DRY MUSTARD
½ CUP SUGAR	1 TEASPOON SALT
1 TABLESPOON GRATED ONION	

In blender, combine oil, vinegar, sugar, onion, poppy seeds, dry mustard, and salt and puree until smooth and thick. Transfer to jar; cover and refrigerate up to 2 days. Stir well before using.

EACH TABLESPOON: ABOUT 99 CALORIES | 0 G PROTEIN | 4 G CARBOHYDRATE | 9 G TOTAL FAT (1 G SATURATED) | 0 MG CHOLESTEROL | 97 MG SODIUM

RANCH DRESSING

Buttermilk gives Ranch Dressing its characteristic tang and creaminess. Use the large holes on a box grater to grate the onion.

ACTIVE TIME: 10 MINUTES · **TOTAL TIME:** 10 MINUTES
MAKES: ABOUT ¾ CUP

½ CUP BUTTERMILK	¼ TEASPOON SALT
⅓ CUP MAYONNAISE	¼ TEASPOON GROUND BLACK PEPPER
2 TABLESPOONS FRESH PARSLEY LEAVES	1 GARLIC CLOVE, CUT IN HALF
½ TEASPOON GRATED ONION	

In blender, combine buttermilk, mayonnaise, parsley, onion, salt, and pepper and puree just until blended. Stir in garlic. Transfer to jar; cover and refrigerate up to 3 days. Remove garlic before serving.

EACH TABLESPOON: ABOUT 48 CALORIES | 0 G PROTEIN | 1 G CARBOHYDRATE | 5 G TOTAL FAT (1 G SATURATED) | 4 MG CHOLESTEROL | 93 MG SODIUM

GREEN GODDESS DRESSING

A touch of anchovy paste is the secret ingredient that gives Green Goddess its distinctive flavor.

ACTIVE TIME: 10 MINUTES · **TOTAL TIME:** 10 MINUTES

MAKES: ABOUT ¾ CUP

½ CUP MAYONNAISE

¼ CUP SOUR CREAM

½ CUP LOOSELY PACKED FRESH PARSLEY LEAVES

1 TABLESPOON RED WINE VINEGAR

1 TEASPOON ANCHOVY PASTE

¼ TEASPOON GROUND BLACK PEPPER

In blender, combine mayonnaise, sour cream, parsley, vinegar, anchovy paste, and pepper. Puree until smooth, scraping down sides of blender occasionally. Transfer to jar; cover and refrigerate up to 3 days.

EACH TABLESPOON: ABOUT 78 CALORIES | 0 G PROTEIN | 1 G CARBOHYDRATE | 8 G TOTAL FAT (2 G SATURATED) | 8 MG CHOLESTEROL | 79 MG SODIUM

From left: Green Goddess and Russian Dressings (page 134)

EASY AÏOLI

Aïoli (ay-OH-lee) is a very garlicky mayonnaise from Provence. We've reduced the garlic's harshness by cooking it. Wonderful as a dip for vegetables or seafood and as a sauce for fish or lamb, it is also the traditional condiment for Bouillabaisse.

ACTIVE TIME: 5 MINUTES · **TOTAL TIME:** 25 MINUTES PLUS COOLING
MAKES: ABOUT ¾ CUP

1⅛ TEASPOONS SALT

1 HEAD GARLIC, SEPARATED INTO CLOVES (ABOUT 14 CLOVES)

½ CUP MAYONNAISE

2 TEASPOONS FRESH LEMON JUICE

½ TEASPOON DIJON MUSTARD

⅛ TEASPOON GROUND RED PEPPER (CAYENNE)

¼ CUP EXTRAVIRGIN OLIVE OIL

1 In 2-quart saucepan, combine 4 cups water and 1 teaspoon salt; heat to boiling. Add garlic and boil until garlic has softened, about 20 minutes. Drain. When cool enough to handle, squeeze soft garlic from each clove into small bowl.

2 In blender, combine garlic, mayonnaise, lemon juice, mustard, remaining ⅛ teaspoon salt, and ground red pepper and puree until smooth. With blender running at low speed and center of cover removed, add oil in slow, steady stream until mixture is thick and creamy. Transfer to small bowl; cover and refrigerate up to 4 hours.

EACH TABLESPOON: ABOUT 112 CALORIES | 0 G PROTEIN | 2 G CARBOHYDRATE | 12 G TOTAL FAT (2 G SATURATED) | 5 MG CHOLESTEROL | 276 MG SODIUM

PESTO

A dollop of this versatile sauce adds so much flavor to soups, such as Minestrone. You can also toss it with cooked potatoes or pasta and even use it as a topping for pizza. Pesto freezes really well, so you could make up several batches at once, to have on hand when fresh basil is out of season.

ACTIVE TIME: 10 MINUTES · **TOTAL TIME:** 10 MINUTES

MAKES: 1 CUP

1½ CUPS PACKED FRESH BASIL LEAVES

½ CUP FRESHLY GRATED PARMESAN CHEESE

⅓ CUP OLIVE OIL

½ TEASPOON SALT

2 TABLESPOONS WATER

In blender, combine basil, Parmesan, oil, salt, and water and puree until smooth. To store, spoon into a small container and top with a few tablespoons of olive oil. Cover and refrigerate for up to 1 week.

EACH TABLESPOON: ABOUT 52 CALORIES | 1 G PROTEIN | 0 G CARBOHYDRATE | 5 G TOTAL FAT (1 G SATURATED) | 2 MG CHOLESTEROL | 119 MG SODIUM

SALSA VERDE

Our recipe for Italian green sauce makes a terrific spread for fresh mozzarella and tomato sandwiches.

ACTIVE TIME: 15 MINUTES · **TOTAL TIME:** 15 MINUTES

MAKES: ABOUT 1 CUP

1   GARLIC CLOVE, CUT IN HALF

¼   TEASPOON SALT

2   CUPS PACKED FRESH FLAT-LEAF PARSLEY LEAVES (ABOUT 3 BUNCHES)

⅓   CUP OLIVE OIL

3   TABLESPOONS CAPERS, DRAINED

3   TABLESPOONS FRESH LEMON JUICE

1   TEASPOON DIJON MUSTARD

⅛   TEASPOON COARSELY GROUND BLACK PEPPER

In blender, combine garlic, salt, parsley, oil, capers, lemon juice, mustard, and pepper and blend until finely chopped. Transfer to small bowl. If not using sauce right away, cover and refrigerate up to 3 days.

EACH TABLESPOON: ABOUT 60 CALORIES │ 0 G PROTEIN │ 1 G CARBOHYDRATE │ 6 G TOTAL FAT (1 G SATURATED) │ 0 MG CHOLESTEROL │ 140 MG SODIUM

TARTAR SAUCE

Traditionally served with fish or crab cakes, this sauce can also be tossed with canned tuna for a terrific tuna salad or used as a spread for sandwiches.

ACTIVE TIME: 15 MINUTES · **TOTAL TIME:** 15 MINUTES
MAKES: ABOUT ¾ CUP

½ CUP MAYONNAISE

¼ CUP CHOPPED DILL PICKLE

2 TABLESPOONS FRESH PARSLEY LEAVES

2 TEASPOONS MILK

2 TEASPOONS DISTILLED WHITE VINEGAR

½ TEASPOON FINELY CHOPPED ONION

½ TEASPOON DIJON MUSTARD

In blender, combine mayonnaise, pickle, parsley, milk, vinegar, onion, and mustard and blend until parsley and pickle are finely chopped. Transfer to small bowl. If not using sauce right away, cover and refrigerate for up to 2 days.

EACH TABLESPOON: ABOUT 68 CALORIES | 0 G PROTEIN | 1 G CARBOHYDRATE | 7 G TOTAL FAT (1 G SATURATED) | 6 MG CHOLESTEROL | 96 MG SODIUM

HOLLANDAISE SAUCE

Making a hollandaise has always seemed difficult because it is an emulsion that can break down if not heated properly. But making it in the blender actually helps stabilize the sauce. Delicious served with fish, vegetables, and that all-time favorite—Eggs Benedict.

ACTIVE TIME: 5 MINUTES · **TOTAL TIME:** 15 MINUTES
MAKES: 1 CUP

---

3 LARGE EGG YOLKS

¼ CUP WATER

2 TABLESPOONS FRESH LEMON JUICE

¼ TEASPOON SALT

½ CUP BUTTER (1 STICK), MELTED
(DO NOT USE MARGARINE)

1 In heavy nonreactive 1-quart saucepan, with whisk, mix egg yolks, water, lemon juice, and salt until well blended. Cook over medium-low heat, stirring constantly with wooden spoon or heat-safe rubber spatula, until egg-yolk mixture just begins to bubble at edge, 6 to 8 minutes.
2 If necessary, reheat butter until hot. Pour yolk mixture into blender. With blender running at low speed and center of cover removed, add butter in a thin stream, blending until sauce is smooth and slightly thickened. If necessary, return sauce to saucepan, stirring constantly over low heat until hot.

EACH TABLESPOON: ABOUT 65 CALORIES | 1 G PROTEIN | 0 G CARBOHYDRATE | 7 G TOTAL FAT (4 G SATURATED) | 56 MG CHOLESTEROL | 100 MG SODIUM

NO-COOK BERRY SAUCE

Spoon this fast, fresh, jewel-tone topping over ice cream, pound cake, or waffles, or stir a couple of tablespoons into a glass of lemonade for a delicious new drink. The amount of sugar needed depends on the flavor of the fruit, so sweeten to taste—the sauce should retain the natural tanginess and flavor of whichever berry you're using.

ACTIVE TIME: 20 MINUTES · **TOTAL TIME:** 20 MINUTES

MAKES: ABOUT 1½ CUPS

3 CUPS RASPBERRIES, BLACKBERRIES, STRAWBERRIES, OR BLUEBERRIES

½ TO ⅔ CUP CONFECTIONERS' SUGAR, DEPENDING ON SWEETNESS OF BERRIES

1 TO 2 TEASPOONS FRESH LEMON OR LIME JUICE, OR TO TASTE

1 In blender, blend berries until pureed. Sift ½ cup confectioners' sugar over berries; blend until smooth. Press berry mixture through medium-mesh sieve to remove seeds. Discard seeds.

2 Stir in 1 teaspoon lemon or lime juice. Taste and adjust sugar and citrus juice. Cover and refrigerate if not serving immediately. Sauce will thicken upon standing; whisk just before serving if necessary. Keep sauce refrigerated and use within 3 days.

EACH TABLESPOON: ABOUT 15 CALORIES | 0 G PROTEIN | 4 G CARBOHYDRATE | 0 G TOTAL FAT (0 G SATURATED) | 0 MG CHOLESTEROL | 0 MG SODIUM

BLENDER MAYONNAISE

Homemade mayonnaise can't be beat, but since it calls for a raw egg, make sure it's pasteurized.

ACTIVE TIME: 10 MINUTES · **TOTAL TIME:** 10 MINUTES

MAKES: 1¼ CUPS

½ CUP VEGETABLE OIL

1 LARGE PASTEURIZED EGG

2 TABLESPOONS CIDER VINEGAR OR FRESH LEMON JUICE

1 TEASPOON DRY MUSTARD

¾ TEASPOON SALT

½ TEASPOON SUGAR

⅛ TEASPOON WHITE PEPPER

½ CUP OLIVE OIL

1 In blender, combine ¼ cup vegetable oil, egg, vinegar, mustard, salt, sugar, and pepper. Blend until combined.

2 With blender running at low speed and with center of cover (or cover) removed, very slowly pour remaining vegetable oil and olive oil in a steady stream, blending until mixture is thickened and creamy.

EACH TABLESPOON: ABOUT 101 CALORIES | 0 G PROTEIN | 0 G CARBOHYDRATE | 11 G TOTAL FAT (1 G SATURATED) | 11 MG CHOLESTEROL | 90 MG SODIUM

CHIMICHURRI SAUCE

This Argentinean herb vinaigrette is what stands in for steak sauce at Buenos Aires steakhouses. Drizzle it on sandwiches, or serve with grilled or roasted meats.

ACTIVE TIME: 20 MINUTES · **TOTAL TIME:** 20 MINUTES
MAKES: ABOUT 1 CUP

1 LARGE GARLIC CLOVE, MINCED

½ TEASPOON SALT

1½ CUPS LOOSELY PACKED FRESH FLAT-LEAF PARSLEY LEAVES, CHOPPED

1 CUP LOOSELY PACKED FRESH CILANTRO LEAVES

¾ CUP OLIVE OIL

2 TABLESPOONS RED WINE VINEGAR

½ TEASPOON CRUSHED RED PEPPER

1 With side of chef's knife, mash garlic and salt to a smooth paste.

2 In blender, combine garlic mixture, parsley, cilantro, oil, vinegar, and crushed red pepper and blend until combined. Serve, or cover and refrigerate up to 4 hours.

EACH TABLESPOON: ABOUT 93 CALORIES │ 0 G PROTEIN │ 1 G CARBOHYDRATE │ 10 G TOTAL FAT (1 G SATURATED) │ 0 MG CHOLESTEROL │ 76 MG SODIUM

ROASTED GARLIC SAUCE

The garlic may be roasted well in advance, squeezed out of its skin, and refrigerated until you are ready to use it.

ACTIVE TIME: 15 MINUTES · **TOTAL TIME:** 1 HOUR, 15 MINUTES PLUS COOLING

MAKES: 1 CUP

---

2   HEADS GARLIC, NOT PEELED

1   SLICE FIRM WHITE BREAD, TORN
    INTO PIECES

3   TABLESPOONS OLIVE OIL

2   TABLESPOONS SOUR CREAM

2   TEASPOONS FRESH LEMON JUICE

½   TEASPOON SALT

⅓   CUP WATER

1   Preheat oven to 350°F. Remove any loose papery skin from garlic, leaving heads intact. Wrap each garlic head in foil and place in small baking dish. Roast until garlic has softened, about 1 hour. When cool enough to handle, separate garlic into cloves. Squeeze the soft garlic from each clove into a bowl.

2   In blender, blend garlic, bread, oil, sour cream, lemon juice, and salt until smooth. Add water and blend until mixed. Serve, or cover and refrigerate up to 1 day.

EACH TABLESPOON: ABOUT 39 CALORIES │ 1 G PROTEIN │ 3 G CARBOHYDRATE │ 3 G TOTAL FAT (1 G SATURATED) │ 1 MG CHOLESTEROL │ 84 MG SODIUM

SUBLIME CHOCOLATE SAUCE

Chocoholics will find this divine sauce the perfect partner for cakes, ice cream, brownies, and our own chocolate waffles.

ACTIVE TIME: 5 MINUTES · **TOTAL TIME:** 10 MINUTES
MAKES: 2 CUPS

4   SQUARES (4 OUNCES) UNSWEETENED CHOCOLATE

1   CUP HEAVY OR WHIPPING CREAM

¾   CUP SUGAR

2   TABLESPOONS LIGHT CORN SYRUP

2   TABLESPOONS BUTTER OR MARGARINE, CUT UP

2   TEASPOONS VANILLA EXTRACT

1   In blender, pulse chocolate until finely chopped.

2   In 2-quart saucepan, combine cream, sugar, and corn syrup; heat, stirring, to boiling over medium-high heat.

3   Transfer hot cream mixture to blender; add butter and vanilla. With center part of cover removed to allow steam to escape, blend until smooth.

EACH TABLESPOON: ABOUT 73 CALORIES | 1 G PROTEIN | 7 G CARBOHYDRATE | 6 G TOTAL FAT (3 G SATURATED) | 12 MG CHOLESTEROL | 13 MG SODIUM

PANCAKES, POPOVERS & WAFFLES

Overnight Baked French Toast (page 161)

POPOVERS

Feather-light, golden brown popovers are crispy on the outside and hollow on the inside. Include these at your next brunch. Serve them fresh from the oven, or make ahead and reheat in a 400°F oven for fifteen minutes.

ACTIVE TIME: 10 MINUTES · **TOTAL TIME:** 1 HOUR, 10 MINUTES
MAKES: 8 MEDIUM OR 12 SMALL POPOVERS

BUTTER OR VEGETABLE OIL FOR GREASING CUPS	3 TABLESPOONS BUTTER OR MARGARINE, MELTED
3 LARGE EGGS	1 CUP ALL-PURPOSE FLOUR
1 CUP MILK	½ TEASPOON SALT

1 Preheat oven to 375°F. Generously grease eight 6-ounce custard cups or twelve 2½" by 1¼" muffin-pan cups with butter or vegetable oil. Place custard cups in jelly-roll pan for easier handling.
2 In blender, combine eggs, milk, melted butter, flour, and salt and blend until smooth.
3 Pour about ⅓ cup batter into each prepared custard cup, or fill muffin-pan cups half-full. Bake 50 minutes, then, with tip of knife, quickly cut small slit in top of each popover to release steam; bake 10 minutes longer. Immediately remove popovers from cups, loosening with spatula if necessary. Serve hot.

EACH MEDIUM POPOVER: ABOUT 159 CALORIES | 5 G PROTEIN | 14 G CARBOHYDRATE | 9 G TOTAL FAT (5 G SATURATED) | 101 MG CHOLESTEROL | 247 MG SODIUM

GIANT POPOVERS

MAKES: 6 GIANT POPOVERS

Generously grease six deep 8-ounce ceramic custard cups; place in jelly-roll pan. Prepare popovers as directed but use **6 eggs, 2 cups milk, 6 tablespoons butter or margarine, melted, 2 cups flour,** and **1 teaspoon salt.** Bake 1 hour before cutting slit in top of popovers.

BASIC CREPES

These delicate pancakes can be stuffed with fresh berries or rolled up with some jam. The crepes can be prepared up to one day ahead; wrap a stack tightly in plastic wrap and refrigerate.

ACTIVE TIME: 5 MINUTES · **TOTAL TIME:** 30 MINUTES PLUS CHILLING

MAKES: ABOUT 12 CREPES

---

3 LARGE EGGS	⅔ CUP ALL-PURPOSE FLOUR
1½ CUPS MILK	½ TEASPOON SALT
4 TABLESPOONS BUTTER OR MARGARINE, MELTED	

1 In blender, combine eggs, milk, 2 tablespoons butter, flour, and salt and blend until smooth, scraping down sides of blender. Transfer batter to medium bowl; cover and refrigerate at least 1 hour or up to overnight to allow flour to absorb liquid.

2 Heat nonstick 10-inch skillet over medium-high heat. Brush bottom of skillet lightly with some remaining butter. With wire whisk, thoroughly mix batter to blend well. Pour scant ¼ cup batter into skillet; tilt pan to coat bottom completely with batter. Cook crepe until top is set and underside is lightly browned, about 1½ minutes.

3 With heat-safe rubber spatula, loosen edge of crepe; turn. Cook until second side has browned, about 30 seconds. Slip crepe onto waxed paper. Repeat with remaining batter, brushing pan lightly with butter before cooking each crepe and stacking crepes between layers of waxed paper.

EACH CREPE: ABOUT 97 CALORIES | 3 G PROTEIN | 7 G CARBOHYDRATE | 6 G TOTAL FAT (3 G SATURATED) | 68 MG CHOLESTEROL | 166 MG SODIUM

CHERRY-ALMOND CLAFOUTI

A French country specialty, clafouti—or clafoutis—is rather like a thick, fruit-studded pancake. Serve it for breakfast, brunch, or dessert.

ACTIVE TIME: 20 MINUTES · **TOTAL TIME:** ABOUT 1 HOUR, 5 MINUTES
MAKES: 12 SERVINGS

1 POUND DARK SWEET CHERRIES, PITTED

2 CUPS HALF-AND-HALF OR LIGHT CREAM

⅓ CUP GRANULATED SUGAR

2 TABLESPOONS AMARETTO (ALMOND-FLAVORED LIQUEUR)

4 LARGE EGGS

⅔ CUP ALL-PURPOSE FLOUR

CONFECTIONERS' SUGAR

1 Preheat oven to 350°F. Grease 10" by 1½" round ceramic baking dish.

2 Place cherries in prepared dish. In blender, combine half-and-half, granulated sugar, amaretto, eggs, and flour and blend until smooth.

3 Pour egg mixture over cherries in prepared dish. Bake 40 to 45 minutes, until custard is set and knife inserted 1 inch from edge comes out clean (center will still jiggle). Sprinkle with confectioners' sugar. Serve hot.

EACH SERVING: ABOUT 155 CALORIES | 4 G PROTEIN | 20 G CARBOHYDRATE | 7 G TOTAL FAT (4 G SATURATED) | 86 MG CHOLESTEROL | 40 MG SODIUM

PUFFY PANCAKE

This baked pancake, which is really popover batter cooked in a skillet, is a tasty brunch-time treat. If you like, fill it with fresh berries and sliced bananas, or serve with jam or marmalade. Use a skillet made of heavy aluminum or cast iron for best results.

ACTIVE TIME: 15 MINUTES · **TOTAL TIME:** 45 MINUTES
MAKES: 6 MAIN-DISH SERVINGS

4   LARGE EGGS

1   CUP MILK

1   CUP ALL-PURPOSE FLOUR

2   TABLESPOONS GRANULATED SUGAR

¼   TEASPOON SALT

2   TABLESPOONS BUTTER
    OR MARGARINE

CONFECTIONERS' SUGAR

1   Preheat oven to 425°F. In blender, combine eggs, milk, flour, granulated sugar, and salt and blend until smooth.

2   In oven-safe 12-inch skillet (if skillet is not oven-safe, wrap handle with double layer of foil), melt butter in oven. Pour batter into skillet; return to oven and bake until pancake has puffed and is golden, about 15 minutes. Dust with confectioners' sugar and serve hot.

EACH SERVING: ABOUT 200 CALORIES | 8 G PROTEIN | 22 G CARBOHYDRATE | 9 G TOTAL FAT (4 G SATURATED) | 158 MG CHOLESTEROL | 197 MG SODIUM

PUFFY APPLE PANCAKE

Caramelized apples are an easy, delicious, and nutritious way to enhance our basic puffy pancake.

ACTIVE TIME: 15 MINUTES · **TOTAL TIME:** 45 MINUTES

MAKES: 6 MAIN-DISH SERVINGS

---

2   TABLESPOONS BUTTER
     OR MARGARINE

½   CUP PLUS 2 TABLESPOONS SUGAR

¼   CUP WATER

6   MEDIUM GRANNY SMITH OR
     NEWTOWN PIPPIN APPLES
     (2 POUNDS), EACH PEELED, CORED,
     AND CUT INTO 8 WEDGES

3   LARGE EGGS

¾   CUP MILK

¾   CUP ALL-PURPOSE FLOUR

¼   TEASPOON SALT

1   Preheat oven to 425°F. In oven-safe 12-inch skillet (if skillet is not oven-safe, wrap handle with double layer of foil), combine butter, ½ cup sugar, and water; heat to boiling over medium-high heat. Add apples and cook, stirring occasionally, until apples are golden and sugar mixture begins to caramelize, about 15 minutes.

2   Meanwhile, in blender, combine eggs, milk, flour, remaining 2 tablespoons sugar, and salt and blend until smooth.

3   Pour batter over apples. Place skillet in oven and bake until pancake has puffed and is golden, about 15 minutes. Serve hot.

EACH SERVING: ABOUT 301 CALORIES | 6 G PROTEIN | 54 G CARBOHYDRATE | 8 G TOTAL FAT (4 G SATURATED) | 121 MG CHOLESTEROL | 181 MG SODIUM

CHEESE BLINTZES

This New York City favorite is similar to a crepe, but cooked with a rich, creamy cheese filling. We accented ours with a hint of orange. Great for breakfast, brunch, or a light supper, they freeze well so they can be made ahead.

ACTIVE TIME: 25 MINUTES · **TOTAL TIME:** 37 MINUTES PLUS STANDING
MAKES: 12 BLINTZES OR 4 SERVINGS

¾ CUP PLUS 2 TABLESPOONS MILK

2 LARGE EGGS

3 TABLESPOONS BUTTER OR MARGARINE, MELTED

½ CUP ALL-PURPOSE FLOUR

¼ TEASPOON SALT

1 PACKAGE (7½ OUNCES) FARMER CHEESE

1 PACKAGE (3 OUNCES) CREAM CHEESE, SOFTENED

¼ CUP SUGAR

½ TEASPOON FRESHLY GRATED ORANGE PEEL

1 In blender, combine milk, eggs, and 1 tablespoon of the melted butter and blend. Add flour and salt and blend until just combined. Let stand 20 minutes at room temperature.

2 Meanwhile, in small bowl, with mixer at medium speed, beat farmer cheese, cream cheese, sugar, and orange peel until smooth.

3 Lightly grease nonstick 8-inch skillet and heat over medium heat. Stir batter; pour about 2 tablespoons into skillet. Tilt pan to coat bottom completely with batter. Cook pancake until top is set and underside is lightly browned, about 1 minute. Invert pancake, browned side up, onto waxed paper. Repeat with remaining batter, stacking pancakes between layers of waxed paper and greasing skillet as needed. Cool to room temperature.

4 Place 12 pancakes, browned side up, on surface. Spoon scant 2 tablespoons cheese mixture into center of each pancake. Fold two opposite sides over to enclose filling. Fold sides in.

5 In 12-inch skillet, heat half of remaining butter over medium heat. Place 6 blintzes, seam side down, in pan and cook, turning once, until lightly browned, 6 minutes. Repeat with remaining butter and blintzes. Serve hot.

EACH SERVING: ABOUT 529 CALORIES | 21 G PROTEIN | 29 G CARBOHYDRATE | 37 G TOTAL FAT (12 G SATURATED) | 211 MG CHOLESTEROL | 601 MG SODIUM

YORKSHIRE PUDDING

This savory English classic is traditionally served with roast beef and made from the pan drippings. Reminiscent of a giant popover, it puffs up golden and brown while baking. It would also be great made from roast pork or bacon drippings.

ACTIVE TIME: 5 MINUTES · **TOTAL TIME:** 30 MINUTES
MAKES: 8 SERVINGS

---

3 TABLESPOONS DRIPPINGS FROM ROAST (SUCH AS ROAST BEEF)

1½ CUPS MILK

3 LARGE EGGS

1½ CUPS ALL-PURPOSE FLOUR

¾ TEASPOON SALT

1 Preheat oven to 450°F. Pour drippings into a 13" by 9" metal baking pan; bake 2 minutes.

2 Meanwhile, in blender, combine milk and eggs and blend. Add flour and salt and blend until mixture is just combined.

3 Remove pan from oven and pour batter over drippings. Bake until puffed and lightly browned, about 25 minutes. Cut into squares.

EACH SERVING: ABOUT 180 CALORIES | 7 G PROTEIN | 20 G CARBOHYDRATE | 8 G TOTAL FAT (3 G SATURATED) | 91 MG CHOLESTEROL | 267 MG SODIUM

OVERNIGHT BAKED FRENCH TOAST

With its glorious brown sugar crust, this rich, eggy French toast is a beautiful choice for company—and it's made with very little effort. Garnish with a sprinkling of confectioners' sugar and fresh berries.

ACTIVE TIME: 10 MINUTES · **TOTAL TIME:** 1 HOUR, 10 MINUTES PLUS CHILLING
MAKES: 8 SERVINGS

12 SLICES FIRM WHITE BREAD

6 LARGE EGGS

2 CUPS MILK

1 TEASPOON VANILLA EXTRACT

¼ TEASPOON GROUND CINNAMON

¼ TEASPOON GROUND NUTMEG

PINCH SALT

½ CUP PACKED BROWN SUGAR

4 TABLESPOONS BUTTER OR MARGARINE, SOFTENED

1 TABLESPOON MAPLE SYRUP

1 Arrange bread slices in four stacks in 8-inch square baking dish.

2 In blender, combine eggs, milk, vanilla, cinnamon, nutmeg, and salt and blend until mixture is smooth. Slowly pour egg mixture over bread slices; press bread down to absorb egg mixture, spooning egg mixture over any uncoated bread. Cover and refrigerate overnight.

3 Preheat oven to 350°F. In small bowl, stir brown sugar, butter, and maple syrup until combined. Spread evenly over each stack of bread. Bake until knife inserted 1 inch from center comes out clean, about 1 hour. Let stand 15 minutes before serving.

EACH SERVING: ABOUT 308 CALORIES | 10 G PROTEIN | 37 G CARBOHYDRATE | 13 G TOTAL FAT (6 G SATURATED) | 184 MG CHOLESTEROL, 364 MG SODIUM

BUTTERMILK PANCAKES

A light and tender pancake with a mild tang. If you don't have buttermilk, use plain low-fat yogurt combined with milk; it will be just as
good.

ACTIVE TIME: 10 MINUTES · **TOTAL TIME PER BATCH:** 4 MINUTES

MAKES: 12 PANCAKES OR 3 SERVINGS

1¼ CUPS BUTTERMILK

3 TABLESPOONS BUTTER OR
  MARGARINE, MELTED

1 LARGE EGG

1 CUP ALL-PURPOSE FLOUR

2 TABLESPOONS SUGAR

2 TEASPOONS BAKING POWDER

½ TEASPOON BAKING SODA

½ TEASPOON SALT

VEGETABLE OIL FOR BRUSHING PAN

1 In blender, combine buttermilk, butter, and egg and blend. Add flour,
sugar, baking powder, baking soda, and salt and blend just until combined.
2 Heat griddle or 12-inch skillet over medium heat until drop of water
sizzles; brush lightly with oil. Pour batter by ¼ cups onto hot griddle, making a few pancakes at a time. Cook until tops are bubbly and edges look
dry. With wide spatula, turn and cook until underside is golden. Transfer to
platter; keep warm.
3 Repeat with the remaining batter, brushing the griddle with more vegetable oil as necessary.

EACH SERVING: ABOUT 369 CALORIES | 10 G PROTEIN | 46 G CARBOHYDRATE | 16 G TOTAL
FAT (9 G SATURATED) | 107 MG CHOLESTEROL | 1,113 MG SODIUM

CLASSIC PANCAKES

The blender makes it easy to whip up pancakes from scratch. If you prefer thinner pancakes, use a little more milk.

ACTIVE TIME: 10 MINUTES · **TOTAL TIME PER BATCH:** 4 MINUTES

MAKES: 12 PANCAKES OR 3 SERVINGS

1¼ CUPS MILK

3 TABLESPOONS BUTTER OR MARGARINE, MELTED

1 LARGE EGG

1 CUP ALL-PURPOSE FLOUR

2 TABLESPOONS SUGAR

2½ TEASPOONS BAKING POWDER

½ TEASPOON SALT

VEGETABLE OIL FOR BRUSHING PAN

1 In blender, combine milk, butter, and egg and blend. Add flour, sugar, baking powder, and salt and blend just until combined.

2 Heat griddle or 12-inch skillet over medium heat until drop of water sizzles; brush lightly with oil. Pour batter by ¼ cups onto hot griddle, making a few pancakes at a time. Cook until tops are bubbly and edges look dry. With wide spatula, turn and cook until underside is golden. Transfer to platter; keep warm.

3 Repeat with the remaining batter, brushing the griddle with more vegetable oil as necessary.

EACH SERVING: ABOUT 391 CALORIES | 10 G PROTEIN | 46 G CARBOHYDRATE | 18 G TOTAL FAT (10 G SATURATED) | 117 MG CHOLESTEROL | 912 MG SODIUM

BLUEBERRY PANCAKES

Prepare as directed but stir **1 cup blueberries** into batter just before cooking.

BUCKWHEAT PANCAKES

Prepare as directed but use **½ cup all-purpose flour** and **½ cup buckwheat flour**.

BANANA PANCAKES

Prepare as directed but add **1 very ripe medium banana, mashed (about ½ cup)**, and **¼ teaspoon baking soda**; use only **¾ cup milk**.

CORNMEAL PANCAKES

Prepare as directed but add **¼ cup cornmeal** to blender along with flour mixture.

SOUR CREAM PANCAKES

Substitute plain or vanilla yogurt if you don't have sour cream on hand. For a spectacular topping, place some fresh blueberries on top, drizzle with blueberry syrup, then dust with confectioners' sugar pushed through a fine-meshed sieve.

ACTIVE TIME: 10 MINUTES · **TOTAL TIME PER BATCH:** 3 TO 4 MINUTES
MAKES: 16 PANCAKES OR 4 SERVINGS

1 CONTAINER (8 OUNCES) SOUR CREAM	2 TABLESPOONS SUGAR
½ CUP MILK	2 TEASPOONS BAKING POWDER
3 TABLESPOONS BUTTER OR MARGARINE, MELTED	½ TEASPOON BAKING SODA
1 LARGE EGG	½ TEASPOON SALT
1 CUP ALL-PURPOSE FLOUR	VEGETABLE OIL FOR BRUSHING PAN

1 In blender, combine sour cream, milk, butter, and egg and blend. Add flour, sugar, baking powder, baking soda, and salt and blend just until combined, scraping blender with spatula if necessary.

2 Heat griddle or 12-inch skillet over medium heat until drop of water sizzles; brush lightly with oil. Pour batter by scant ¼ cups onto hot griddle, making a few pancakes at a time. Cook until tops are bubbly and edges look dry. With wide spatula, turn and cook until underside is golden. Transfer to platter; keep warm.

3 Repeat with the remaining batter, brushing the griddle with more vegetable oil as necessary.

EACH SERVING: ABOUT 388 CALORIES | 8 G PROTEIN | 34 G CARBOHYDRATE | 25 G TOTAL FAT (14 G SATURATED) | 107 MG CHOLESTEROL | 800 MG SODIUM

BUTTERMILK WAFFLES

Crisp yet fluffy, these are worth getting out of bed for. Top with butter, syrup, or your favorite fresh fruit.

ACTIVE TIME: 10 MINUTES · **TOTAL TIME PER BATCH:** 3 TO 4 MINUTES
MAKES: ABOUT 11 WAFFLES OR 4 SERVINGS

2   CUPS BUTTERMILK

4   TABLESPOONS BUTTER OR
    MARGARINE, MELTED

2   LARGE EGGS

1¾ CUPS ALL-PURPOSE FLOUR

1½ TEASPOONS BAKING POWDER

1   TEASPOON BAKING SODA

½   TEASPOON SALT

1   Preheat waffle baker as manufacturer directs. In blender, combine buttermilk, butter, and eggs and blend. Add flour, baking powder, baking soda, and salt and blend until smooth.

2   When waffle baker is ready, pour in batter. Cover and bake as manufacturer directs; do not lift cover during baking.

3   When waffle is done, lift cover and loosen waffle with fork. Serve waffles immediately with butter and maple syrup, or keep warm in oven (place waffle directly on oven before pouring in more batter. If batter becomes too thick upon standing, thin with a little more buttermilk.

EACH SERVING: ABOUT 396 CALORIES │ 13 G PROTEIN │ 48 G CARBOHYDRATE │ 16 G TOTAL FAT (9 G SATURATED) │ 143 MG CHOLESTEROL │ 1,038 MG SODIUM

CHOCOLATE WAFFLES

Who said waffles were just for breakfast? Flavored with vanilla and cocoa powder, this rich chocolate waffle becomes a sundae when topped with vanilla ice cream and our Sublime Chocolate Sauce.

ACTIVE TIME: 15 MINUTES · **TOTAL TIME PER BATCH:** 4 MINUTES
MAKES: 12 WAFFLES OR 4 SERVINGS

2 CUPS MILK

4 TABLESPOONS BUTTER OR MARGARINE, MELTED

2 LARGE EGGS

2 TEASPOONS VANILLA EXTRACT

2 CUPS ALL-PURPOSE FLOUR

1 CUP SUGAR

½ CUP UNSWEETENED COCOA POWDER

1½ TEASPOONS BAKING POWDER

1 TEASPOON BAKING SODA

½ TEASPOON SALT

VANILLA ICE CREAM

SUBLIME CHOCOLATE SAUCE (PAGE 148)

1 Preheat waffle baker as manufacturer directs. In blender, combine milk, butter, eggs, and vanilla and blend. Add flour, sugar, cocoa, baking powder, baking soda, and salt and blend just until combined.

2 When waffle baker is ready, pour in batter. Cover and bake as manufacturer directs; do not lift cover during baking.

3 When waffle is done, lift cover and loosen waffle with fork. Serve immediately with vanilla ice cream and chocolate sauce, or keep warm in oven (place waffle directly on oven rack to keep crisp). Reheat waffle baker before pouring in more batter.

EACH SERVING: ABOUT 664 CALORIES | 16 G PROTEIN | 108 G CARBOHYDRATE | 21 G TOTAL FAT (12 G SATURATED) | 156 MG CHOLESTEROL | 973 MG SODIUM

BUCKWHEAT BLINI

These small Russian pancakes, traditionally served with sour cream and caviar, make a delicious, simple dessert. Drizzle on a little melted butter, then spread on your favorite jam and top with a dollop of sour cream, crème fraîche, or whipped cream. If you like, you can substitute all-purpose flour for the buckwheat.

ACTIVE TIME: 5 MINUTES · **TOTAL TIME PER BATCH:** 2 MINUTES
MAKES: 6 DOZEN OR 8 SERVINGS

½ CUP MILK

1 LARGE EGG

2 TABLESPOONS SOUR CREAM

1 TABLESPOON BUTTER OR
MARGARINE, MELTED

½ CUP BUCKWHEAT FLOUR

¼ CUP ALL-PURPOSE FLOUR

VEGETABLE OIL FOR BRUSHING PAN

1 In blender, combine milk, egg, sour cream, and butter and blend. Add buckwheat flour and all-purpose flour and blend just until combined.
2 Heat griddle or 10-inch skillet over medium heat until a drop of water sizzles; brush lightly with oil. Pour batter by teaspoonfuls onto hot griddle, making 7 or 8 pancakes. Cook until tops are bubbly and edges look dry. With spatula, turn and cook until the undersides are golden. Transfer to platter; keep warm.
3 Repeat with remaining batter, brushing griddle with more vegetable oil if necessary.

EACH SERVING: ABOUT 82 CALORIES | 3 G PROTEIN | 9 G CARBOHYDRATE | 4 G TOTAL FAT (2 G SATURATED) | 34 MG CHOLESTEROL | 33 MG SODIUM

WHOLE-GRAIN WAFFLES

Healthful and delicious, these extra-crunchy waffles get a hint of sweetness from the honey and extra fiber from the whole-wheat flour.

ACTIVE TIME: 10 MINUTES · **TOTAL TIME PER BATCH:** 3 TO 4 MINUTES
MAKES: ABOUT 8 WAFFLES OR 4 SERVINGS

1½ CUPS MILK

4 TABLESPOONS BUTTER OR MARGARINE, MELTED

2 LARGE EGGS

2 TABLESPOONS HONEY

1 CUP ALL-PURPOSE FLOUR

½ CUP WHOLE-WHEAT FLOUR

¼ CUP CORNMEAL

1 TABLESPOON BAKING POWDER

½ TEASPOON SALT

1 Preheat waffle baker as manufacturer directs. In blender, combine milk, butter, eggs, and honey and blend. Add all-purpose flour, whole-wheat flour, cornmeal, baking powder, and salt and blend until mixture is smooth. Let batter stand for 5 minutes.

2 When waffle baker is ready, pour in batter. Cover and bake as manufacturer directs; do not lift cover during baking.

3 When waffle is done, lift cover and loosen waffle with fork. Serve immediately with butter and maple syrup, or keep warm in oven (place waffle directly on oven rack to keep crisp). Reheat waffle baker before pouring in more batter.

EACH SERVING: ABOUT 430 CALORIES | 12 G PROTEIN | 55 G CARBOHYDRATE | 19 G TOTAL FAT (10 G SATURATED) | 152 MG CHOLESTEROL | 791 MG SODIUM

INDEX

THE GOOD HOUSEKEEPING TRIPLE-TEST PROMISE

At Good Housekeeping, we want to make sure that every recipe we print works in any oven, with any brand of ingredient, no matter what. That's why, in our test kitchens at the **Good Housekeeping Research Institute**, we go all out: We test each recipe at least three times—and, often, several more times after that.

When a recipe is first developed, one member of our team prepares the dish and we judge it on these criteria: it must be **delicious, family-friendly, healthy,** and **easy to make.**

1. The recipe is then tested several more times to fine-tune the flavor and ease of preparation, always by the same team member, using the same equipment.

2. Next, another team member follows the recipe as written, **varying the brands of ingredients** and **kinds of equipment.** Even the types of stoves we use are changed.

3. A third team member repeats the whole process **using yet another set of equipment** and **alternative ingredients.**

By the time the recipes appear on these pages, they are guaranteed to work in any kitchen, including yours. WE PROMISE.